Ships In Bottles

Build Your Own Scale Model of a Legendary Ship in a Bottle

F.R. BERCHEM

FOUNTAIN PRESS

First published in 1989 by
Fountain Press Limited
45 The Broadway
Tolworth
Surrey KT6 7DW
England
Published in Canada by
Stoddart Publishing Co. Limited

BRITISH LIBRARY CATALOGUING IN PUBLICATION DATA
Berchem, F.R. (Frederick R.)
    Ships in bottles: build your own scale model of a legendary ship in a bottle.

ISBN 0-86343-006-6

1. Model ships in bottles. Construction - Manuals. I. Title

745.592'.8

Printed and bound in Canada

COVER DESIGN: Brant Cowie/Arts Plus Limited
COVER PHOTOGRAPHS: Exakto Graphics

Contents

Preface

I learned the art of putting ships into bottles from an old Scottish shipmaster when I was in my mid-teens. With all of the misapplied enthusiasm of that age, I made three models that ended in disaster, each one looking like a stage in the progressive destruction of the schooner *Hesperus*.

Finally, while I was a cadet in the old freighter *Wellpark* wallowing across the Bay of Biscay bound for Newcastle upon Tyne in the winter of 1952, I succeeded in putting a ship into a bottle. The rigging hung slack and the sails lay askew as though they had been trimmed by drunken soldiers, but at least the masts were up and straight, and nothing had actually been broken; it was a beginning.

During my next voyage, in the m/v *Lylepark*, I bottled a seamanlike model of a four-masted barque hauling out to sea under full sail. This was completed while the *Lylepark* was loading timber at New Westminster, British Columbia in the summer of 1952, and carried home triumphantly.

The pinnacle of achievement was reached with what I hoped was a recognizable replica of the *Cutty Sark* suitably set in a Haig's Scotch "dimple" bottle. The model was made when I was third officer in the old *Garvelpark* creaking down to West Africa for iron ore at the end of 1953. I gave it away when I was a sub-lieutenant on courses in Portsmouth, and then remembered that I had kept no notes on how to make it.

I have always regarded the full-rigged ship with all sails set and displayed in a Haig's dimple ("pinch") bottle to be the finest example of the types of ships in bottles. As a result, I have made several such models over the years and compiled a set of notes for my guidance and for improvement in successive models. From this basic design other types of ships could also be made.

The skill is not acquired without disappointment, frustration, and the endless patience to overcome them. Craftsmanship and care, the willingness to take risks and to experiment, sureness of eye and hand are all essential for the production of a first-class model. There are no shortcuts and no guaranteed fixes.

In a book about Victoriana the author who described ships in bottles as a mild curiosity for the Sunday diversion of ladies and small children was well wide of the mark; they were, and remain, collectibles for connoisseurs and ship lovers.

I. MAKING A SHIP IN A BOTTLE

Choosing The Model

The sources of inspiration for a model are endless. There are the famous ships of history, the *Nonsuch*, the *Golden Hind*, the *Cutty Sark*; the ships of poems and legends, the vanished and the cursed, like the *Wanderer* and the *Flying Dutchman*; the vessels from the old sea shanties, vessels of all rigs and types, clippers, windjammers, schooners, Arctic whalers, Atlantic liners, traders, coasters, ketches and yawls.

Among my own favorites are the *Loch Achray*, the doomed clipper of John Masefield's epic poem, and the *Phantom Clipper*, sailed by a crew of dead men killed by "Yellow Jack" fever, the dreaded plague of the South American ports. Another favorite is the lateen-rigged, extremely graceful polacre, the very fast trading vessel type sailed by the French in the Mediterranean during the eighteenth century.

Any of these vessels can be made for a pinch bottle using and adapting the dimensions of length, breadth and depth given in the following instructions for building a full-rigged ship.

F.R.B.

THE BOTTLE

First, and most important, obtain the bottle; for this particular model a Haig's dimple (pinch) bottle is used.

The materials which I use are the simplest: a piece of teak wood, wooden matchsticks, a good penknife, three grades of sandpaper (coarse, medium, fine), a small darning needle, black, and sometimes brown, cotton thread and a piece of beeswax and a good bonding glue.

Paints, varnishes, oils and stains may be chosen and applied as desired.

Some model builders use mechanical appliances such as dental drills and needles to make the holes in the hull and masts, but that is a matter of choice.

HULL

Cut a piece of teak to the approximate length, breadth and depth shown:

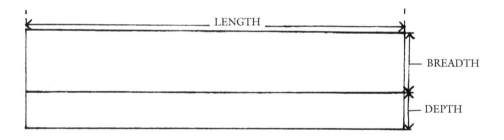

The clipper ship hulls, notably those of Mackay of Boston, were remarkable for the grace and beauty of their lines, and the model should be carved accordingly. Do not merely hack out a pointed end and a round end from the piece of teak.

With a penknife and very coarse sandpaper shape the hull to the outlines shown:

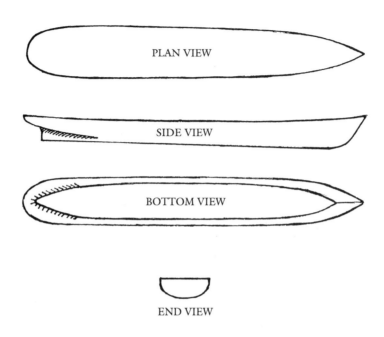

PLAN VIEW

SIDE VIEW

BOTTOM VIEW

END VIEW

END VIEW FROM BOW

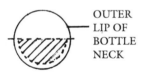

OUTER
LIP OF
BOTTLE
NECK

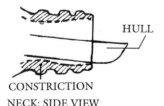

HULL

CONSTRICTION
NECK: SIDE VIEW

Now test the hull to see if it will fit down the neck of the bottle — it should.

Carefully work over the hull with fine sandpaper, gradually trimming the shape to the flowing lines of the clipper ship, and keeping the keel narrow and rounded.

Most important, be sure that the hull will fit into the neck of the bottle with a good clearance. If this is not checked carefully, it may be impossible, later, to push the completed model past the neck.

The midship section of the hull (shaded area) should reach to approximately the level shown against the outer lip of the bottle neck. Bear in mind that the neck constricts slightly before merging into the body of the bottle.

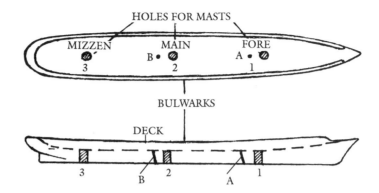

Now carve out the body of the hull, with a penknife or a very fine chisel, to form the deck and bulwarks. Again this must be done with great care because the bulwarks must be thin enough to pass a needle through and yet not be split while they are being shaped, nor when the needle is being passed through them.

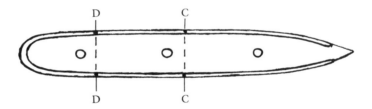

HOLES IN HULL

 (i) Bore holes for the masts right through the deck at the points shown in the diagram (1, 2, 3).
 (ii) Behind the fore and main masts bore holes at a slight angle, down and forward, at *a* and *b* in the diagram. These holes will be for the thread stays to pull up the masts when the ship is in the bottle.
 (iii) Through the bulwarks and as close to the deck level as possible, bore two holes at *c* and *d* in the diagram. These holes

will be for the thread braces that trim the main and fore courses when the ship is in the bottle.

* Great care must be taken when boring these holes, otherwise the wood may split and ruin the model.

When the holes have been bored, lightly oil the hull with teak or linseed oil. After the hull has dried, paint it with clear varnish or with the particular color chosen for the hull.

THE BOWSPRIT

To form the bowsprit, glue two matchsticks together as shown. White glue does an adequate job.

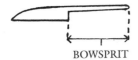

BOWSPRIT

Shape the matchsticks to the dimensions shown above with fine sandpaper, with the bowsprit section being well rounded. Apply a teak or walnut stain.

Because of the rigging lines that will eventually be led through the bowsprit, it must be strong enough to stand considerable strain while the masts are being raised after the ship has been put into the bottle.

To strengthen the bowsprit:

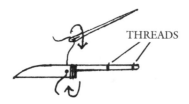

THREADS

Carefully pull a threaded needle through the wood at the point shown, then bind the thread tightly around and finish off by pulling the threaded needle through the wood once more and pulling tight.

Tie a single piece of thread with a reef knot tightly around a point close to the end of the bowsprit. Tie another thread in the same way at the mid-point of the bowsprit.

Varnish the entire section, including the threads, and set to dry.

Sand down the hull with very fine sandpaper and varnish or paint the outer hull and the inside of the bulwarks as desired for the final color scheme. The deck should remain varnished.

Glue the bowsprit section in place and when the glue has dried, varnish the entire bowsprit again, applying the varnish more heavily around the area where the bowsprit section is attached to the deck.

Remember, there will be considerable strain on the bowsprit in the final stages.

Bore holes with a needle as shown through the bowsprit. The needle must be eased rather than forced through, to avoid splitting the narrow bowsprit. The threads around the bowsprit will also help prevent splitting.

If desired, a waterline "boot-topping" can be painted around the hull — dark green, black or dark red are good colors — using masking tape to obtain a clean line.

Pierce a needle hole through the stern on the center line at *2* as shown.

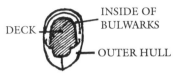

DECK — INSIDE OF BULWARKS

OUTER HULL

EXTRA VARNISH

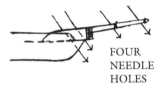

FOUR NEEDLE HOLES

2

BOOT-TOPPING

MASTS

FOREMAST

Choose three matchsticks that are straight, even, and not likely

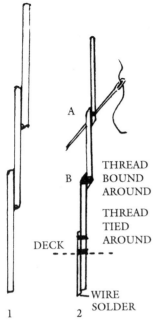

A

B

THREAD
BOUND
AROUND

THREAD
TIED
AROUND

DECK

WIRE
SOLDER

1   2

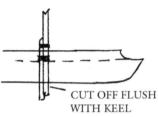

CUT OFF FLUSH
WITH KEEL

MIZZEN   MAIN

to splinter easily — usually those with a healthy, "white" look to them — and glue them together as shown in *1*.

Remembering that the clipper ship was the age of sail's triumph in graceful lines, and not a bargee's nightmare, pare down the mast with a penknife and very fine sandpaper to the proportions shown in *2*.

Bore very cautiously with a needle and thread through the mast at the points shown, *a* and *b*, then bind the thread tightly around the mast to give added strength.

Take a piece of wire, or preferably a short length of wire solder, glue it to the back of the mast and then tie tightly in place with threads where shown. I use a series of overhand knots from side to side. Leave a clear space between the bottom threads — the reason for this will be evident later.

Stain the complete mast with teak or walnut stain.

Set the mast, well glued at its base, into the hole already made in the deck, forcing it down until the lower band of thread is pressing against the deck. Be sure that the mast is standing straight and aligned.

Cut off the protruding end of the mast flush with the keel.

Varnish the entire mast with a slightly heavier application at the base where it touches the deck.

The main and mizzen masts are completed in the same way, to the dimensions shown, fitted in the hull and varnished.

Cut and trim matchsticks for the yards/spars for the fore and mainmasts to the dimensions shown. The yards for the mizzen mast should be very slightly smaller. Stain and varnish the yards/spars and set them to dry.

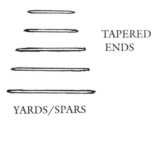

TAPERED
ENDS

YARDS/SPARS

RIGGING

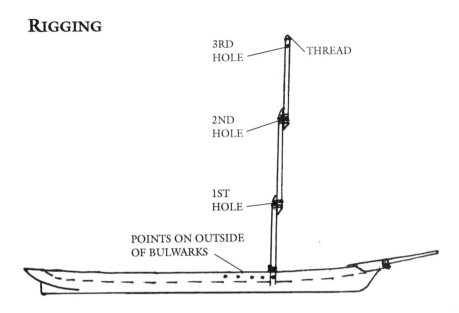

3RD HOLE
THREAD
2ND HOLE
1ST HOLE
POINTS ON OUTSIDE OF BULWARKS

Mark five points along the outsides of the port and starboard bulwarks on either side of the masts as shown.

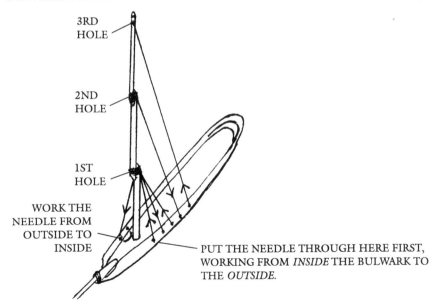

3RD HOLE
2ND HOLE
1ST HOLE
WORK THE NEEDLE FROM OUTSIDE TO INSIDE
PUT THE NEEDLE THROUGH HERE FIRST, WORKING FROM *INSIDE* THE BULWARK TO THE *OUTSIDE*.

Take a long length of thread, approximately 20 inches (50 cm), and rub it with beeswax. Tie a small knot in the end of the thread, then with a needle carefully work the thread through the bulwark at the farthest forward point until the knot comes up against the inside of the bulwark.

Lead the thread up and work the needle through the foremast at the position marked first hole. Pull the thread taut, then come down and work the needle through the farthest forward point on the opposite bulwark from the outside to the inside, and pull taut.

Work the needle and thread through the second point on the same side from the inside to the outside and pull taut. Lead up and through the first hole again and down to the second point on the other side, and work the needle and thread through the bulwark from the outside to the inside.

Continue to the third point on the inside of the bulwark and work to the outside and up through the first hole once more to the opposite bulwark. The first three strands of rigging — the shrouds — now pass through the first hole.

Proceed in the same way through the fourth points and the second hole, to the fifth points and the third hole, so rigging the two sets of stays.

To finish off the rigging, work the needle and thread around the bulwark through the fifth and last point for a second time, pull taut and cut off the thread close to the inside of the bulwark.

Repeat the procedure for the main and mizzen masts.

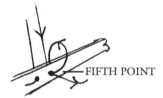
FIFTH POINT

FORE AND AFT RIGGING

The threads for the fore and aft rigging must be rubbed thoroughly with beeswax, and be long enough to lead a short distance out of the bottle neck when the ship is inside the bottle.

Number these threads very carefully, to be sure of which one to pull while raising the masts in the bottle.

Tie the first length of thread — approximately 12 inches (30 cm) long — at the top of the foremast, and with the needle lead it down and through the fore end of the bowsprit behind the

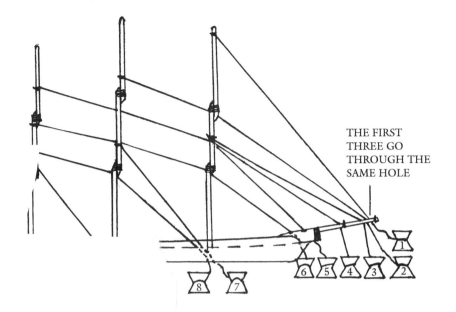

THE FIRST
THREE GO
THROUGH THE
SAME HOLE

around the end. Wrap the loose end of
piece of card clearly marked *1*, and let
owsprit.
— slightly longer than the first — on
est point shown in the diagram and with
the foremast as shown and lead the
n the same hole in the bowsprit as *1*.

slightly longer than the second — on
ighest point shown in the diagram and
ole in the mainmast as shown and lead
e foremast; bore a hole there as shown
and lead the thread down and through the bowsprit at a point
behind the middle thread tied around the bowsprit. Mark this
pull-thread *4* (the reason for this will be clear in the next step).

Take a doubly long length of thread and "middle" it with a reef knot around the foremast, very close above the point at which pull-thread *4* goes through the mast.

Take one loose end of the "middled" thread and with the needle lead it through the first hole in the bowsprit with pull-threads *1* and *2*. Mark this pull-thread *3*.

Take the other loose end and thread it through the third hole in the bowsprit. Mark this pull-thread *5*.

Tie a thread — approximately 15 inches (38 cm) long — around the mizzen mast below the one already tied there — pull-thread *4* — as shown, then lead it forward and with the needle thread it through the mainmast, on through the foremast and down through the fourth hole in the bowsprit to come out through the bow. Mark this pull-thread *6*.

Tie a thread — approximately 14 inches (36 cm) long — around the mainmast very close below where pull-thread *6* passes through it, then with a needle thread through hole *a* in the deck. Mark this pull-thread *7*.

Another long thread is tied around the mizzen mast where shown below the two already tied there and then threaded through the mainmast and down through hole *a*. Mark this pull-thread *8*.

The final thread is tied around the mizzen mast below the other three and is threaded through hole *b* in the deck. Mark this pull-thread *9*.

Do not lose the numberings on the pull-threads because they are essential when pulling up the masts from outside the bottle.

RIGGING THE SPANKER AND GAFF BOOMS — MIZZEN MAST
The spanker and gaff booms are cut and shaped from matchsticks to the dimensions shown, stained and varnished.

Tie threads tightly around the ends that will be next to the mast.

Take a length of thread and with the needle lead it through the boom as shown until the thread is middled; tie it in a reef

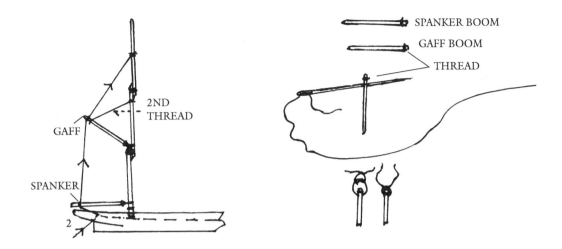

2ND THREAD

GAFF

SPANKER

2

SPANKER BOOM

GAFF BOOM

THREAD

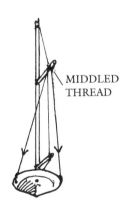

MIDDLED THREAD

knot across the end of the boom and glue in place.

Secure the booms to the mizzen mast by tying the ends around the mast at the heights shown with reef knots.

Take a length of waxed thread and knot one end of it. With the needle thread it up through the hole *2* in the stern until the knot comes up tight. Tie the thread around the outboard end of the spanker boom, lead up and tie around the outboard end of the gaff so that the gaff will set at the angle shown. Finish off by tying the thread around the mizzen mast.

Tie a second thread to the mizzen mast and gaff as shown.

"Middle" a length of thread with an overhand knot at the outboard end of the gaff, then lead one end down and thread it through the bulwark from outside to inside, double it through the hole again, glue in position and cut the end off close to the bulwark. Repeat this procedure with the other end on the opposite bulwark.

The standing rigging of shrouds and backstays, and the fore and aft rigging are now complete. Check that nothing has become slack in the process; any slack parts must be rerigged. Remember, rigging can be a tedious, frustrating job.

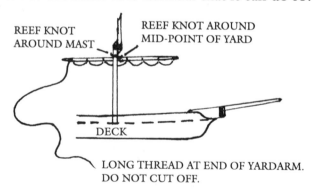

SHORT PIECES OF THREAD

LONG THREAD

FOOT-ROPES

START

TO RIG AND ATTACH THE YARDS

When the yards are completely dry, take a length of waxed cotton thread (sometimes brown thread is used for this rigging) — approximately 9 inches (23 cm) long — and tie one end to the yardarm with a reef knot.

The thread is then gathered up in bights at intervals along the length of the yard with short pieces of thread reef-knotted around it. These bights form the foot-ropes.

The last bight on each yard is formed by tying the long thread with an overhand knot at the other end of the yard, and applying a light touch of glue or varnish.

The end of the thread is then left hanging free for the time being. Do not cut it off.

Mark the exact mid-point of the yard and tie a length of thread around it with a reef knot; glue or varnish lightly and allow to dry.

Starting with the lowest yard on the foremast, attach the yard to the mast at the point shown by tying the thread at the middle of the yard around the mast with a reef knot; glue or varnish lightly after the loose ends have been cut off.

The yard should now be able to swivel about its point of attachment to the mast. It is essential that it can do so.

REEF KNOT AROUND MAST

REEF KNOT AROUND MID-POINT OF YARD

DECK

LONG THREAD AT END OF YARDARM. DO NOT CUT OFF.

Take the long length of thread attached at one end of the yard — at *1* — and thread it with the needle very slowly and cautiously through the mast — it can split very easily if you are hasty —

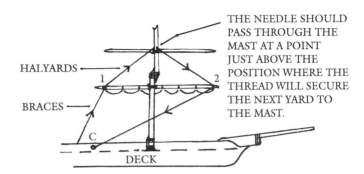

THE NEEDLE SHOULD
PASS THROUGH THE
MAST AT A POINT
JUST ABOVE THE
POSITION WHERE THE
THREAD WILL SECURE
THE NEXT YARD TO
THE MAST.

HALYARDS

BRACES

DECK

at the point shown. Pull the thread taut and tie it around the other end of the yard — at *2* — with an overhand knot and lightly glue in position. When dry, lead the thread aft and with the needle thread it through the hole *c* in the bulwark, across the deck and out through the similar hole in the opposite bulwark, back up to *1*. Pull the thread taut and tie it firmly around the yardarm; glue or varnish lightly, cut off the loose end and allow to dry.

The yard should now be able to pivot horizontally and vertically about its point of attachment.

The remaining yards on the foremast and those on the mainmast are rigged in the same way, and are tied in position on the masts at the heights shown in the following diagram.

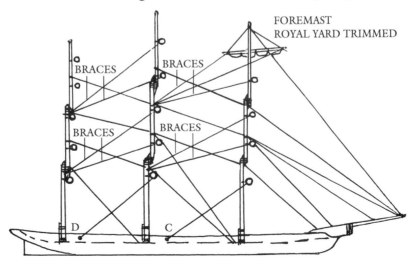

FOREMAST
ROYAL YARD TRIMMED

BRACES   BRACES

BRACES   BRACES

15

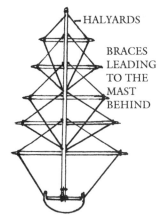
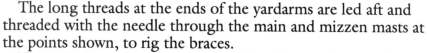

HALYARDS

BRACES
LEADING
TO THE
MAST
BEHIND

NOT TO SCALE/PROPORTION

The long threads at the ends of the yardarms are led aft and threaded with the needle through the main and mizzen masts at the points shown, to rig the braces.

This calls for great care in getting the right tension on the threads. Do not pull them too tightly as the rigging progresses, otherwise those threads already rigged might be slackened. If this happens, the affected parts must be rerigged.

The rigging of the braces on the mizzen mast will be shown in a separate diagram.

When completed, put a light touch of clear varnish at the ends of the yards. This gives an added strength to the slender yards and holds the knots more firmly.

The yards must be positioned so that the fore and aft rigging will pass over them.

RIGGING THE MIZZEN MAST

The yards are rigged similarly to those for the fore and main masts, except that there are no long threads left at the ends of the topgallant and royal yards.

The long thread at the end of the crossjack yard is led aft and with the needle is worked carefully through the bulwark at *E*, led across the deck and through the opposite bulwark and up to the other end of the yard where it is tied, secured, and the end cut off.

The long thread on the lower topsail yard is led forward and with the needle threaded through the mainmast at the point shown and back to the other end of the yard, tied securely and the end cut off.

The procedure is repeated for the upper topsail yard.

The fore and aft and running rigging are now complete. Rigging is a delicate job, especially if the masts and yards are slender, as they should be. Sometimes it may be necessary to dismantle some parts and rerig them.

**Never lead braces forward and down because it would then be impossible to lay the masts backwards to a horizontal position for passing through the bottle neck.

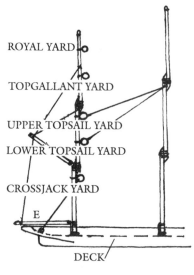

ROYAL YARD

TOPGALLANT YARD

UPPER TOPSAIL YARD

LOWER TOPSAIL YARD

CROSSJACK YARD

E

DECK

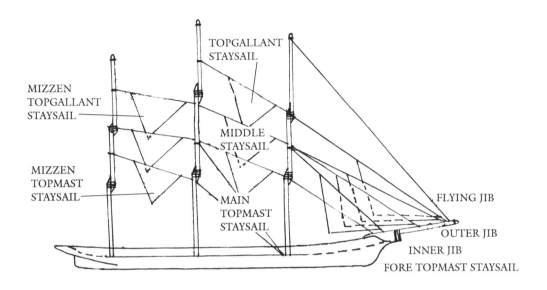

MIZZEN
TOPGALLANT
STAYSAIL

TOPGALLANT
STAYSAIL

MIZZEN
TOPMAST
STAYSAIL

MIDDLE
STAYSAIL

MAIN
TOPMAST
STAYSAIL

FLYING JIB

OUTER JIB

INNER JIB

FORE TOPMAST STAYSAIL

Sails

Because of the difficulty in fitting sails, many models are put into bottles without them. The yards may be left bare; sometimes pieces of gauze bandage or other equally thin material are glued along the yards to give the impression of furled sails.

To make the sails, if it has been decided to fit them, any good quality, plain white paper may be used.

No matter how carefully a model is made according to plans and measurements, discrepancies occur, so that the measurements for the sails must be very accurately made with dividers/calipers, and drawn on paper.

The aim is to create a picture within the bottle, therefore the sails should not be left as plain white paper. They may be tinted and shadowed with watercolors before being fitted in place on the yards with glue; or the lines for reefs and sail sections may be drawn in pencil or ink. A good photograph or painting of a ship under sail can be used as a guide.

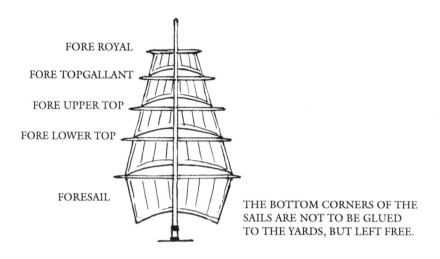

FORE ROYAL

FORE TOPGALLANT

FORE UPPER TOP

FORE LOWER TOP

FORESAIL

THE BOTTOM CORNERS OF THE
SAILS ARE NOT TO BE GLUED
TO THE YARDS, BUT LEFT FREE.

The above diagrams will serve as guides for making the sails —
the jibs and staysails running fore and aft, the square sails on the
yards. The sails and jibs may be curved slightly or bellied as
desired before fitting in place on the yards.

MAIN
TOPMAST

MIZZEN
GAFF

FORE
TOPMAST

FLAGS

Masthead flags may be made and glued in position.

The national ensign is folded and glued around the thread
leading to the mizzen gaff peak.

For accuracy, be sure that the shipping company's house flag
on the mainmast and the national ensign belong to the same
country. The house flag in this case is that of John Willis and
Son, owners of the famous Dumbarton-built clipper, *Cutty Sark*.

The ship is now ready to be put into the bottle.

PREPARING THE BOTTLE

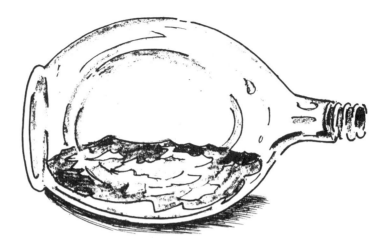

The bottle must be washed out and dried thoroughly, taking care that no cloudy marks are left on the inside.

The bottle may be prepared while the model is being built. To form the sea base, pieces of putty are put into the bottle on the end of a long, flexible wire. A piece of wire coat-hanger can be used for this.

The putty is kneaded into the form of waves using the wire; sometimes pads of masking tape built up on the end of the wire will assist this purpose. Great care must be taken not to smear putty on the sides of the bottle.

When a satisfactory sea has been shaped it is suitably painted with dark blue, dark grey and dark green and white colors to create a realistic effect.

The paint is applied around the trough in which the model will sit; a fine-haired brush attached to the end of a long, flexible wire makes a very good tool for this job.

Mastic putty takes a long time to dry, and may be set in the bottle for at least a week before the model is put in place on the putty.

SETTING THE SHIP IN THE BOTTLE

The pull-threads are unwound on their markers, taking great care that none of the numbered tags come off their respective threads.

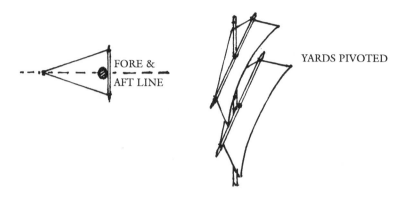

FORE & AFT LINE

YARDS PIVOTED

The yards are trimmed so that they lie at right angles to the fore and aft line of the ship. They are then pivoted to lie along the masts. Be very careful that the rigging does not become fouled.

Very carefully cut three-quarters of the way through the masts between the threads at the base, using a piece of razor blade or a small, very sharp penknife.

The masts are very slowly bent backward until they lie almost flat along the deck.

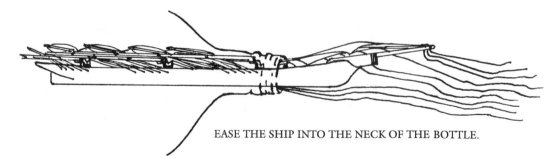

EASE THE SHIP INTO THE NECK OF THE BOTTLE.

No matter how well and how carefully made, the model will be a tight fit, and some pressure will be necessary; it is like giving birth in reverse.

The ends of the yards must be eased very carefully past the mouth; sometimes the model will have to be rotated slightly as it is eased down the neck. A broken yard is almost impossible to fix; a broken mast, unless snapped at the base, can very occasionally be salvaged.

When the hull is past the bottle neck, the operation becomes extremely delicate. It is obvious that the masts must be raised before setting the ship into the putty base, because the top of the mizzen mast will come in contact with the end of the bottle before the hull is completely inside.

To hold the hull suspended while the masts are started up by pulling gently on pull-threads *1*, *2*, *4* and *8*, a pair of forceps-style tweezers may be used. Otherwise, a needle can be firmly secured to the end of a piece of strong wire and stuck in the bow of the ship to hold it as the masts are raised.

The model is now worked down onto the putty while the masts are drawn up by the pull-threads.

It is essential to have at hand the diagram showing all numbered pull-threads and their points of attachment.

From this point on, a considerable amount of nerve and judgment will be needed.

The ship is worked firmly onto the putty, holding it down with a length of wire — again a piece of wire coat-hanger will do — and pulling up the masts to the upright position. Be sure that the main and mizzen masts are fully upright with their shrouds and stays taut, and that pull-threads *7*, *8*, and *9* are also as taut as can be managed.

Light touches of varnish may be applied with the brush where the waterline of the model meets the putty, taking great care that no varnish touches any of the rigging or the pull-threads.

The model can now be left to sit for a week so that it will set solidly in the putty.

When sure that the ship has set firmly in its base, draw pull-threads *1, 2, 3, 4, 5* and *6* as taut as possible, tightening all the rigging and braces. The pull-threads are then glued in position where they pass through the bow and bowsprit. Light weights may be attached to the ends of the pull-threads to keep the strain on them while the glue sets. A touch of varnish may be added on top of the glue. The pull-threads passing underneath the hull are already held firmly in the putty.

With a piece of light wire that can be bent into wondrous shapes and angles, pull the yards into a horizontal position and trim them as desired. When the yards are properly in position, glue the lower corners of the sails in place on the yards below.

RAZOR BLADE SET INTO MATCHSTICK   WIRE

When everything is satisfactorily in position, cut off the ends of all the pull-threads as close as possible to the bowsprit and hull, using a fragment of razor blade securely tied to the end of a wire.

There are some model-makers who claim to set the threads alight and so burn off the loose ends, the flames being extinguished at the critical moment by putting the cap on the bottle, thus cutting off the air supply.

The result, however, is liable to be a fairly vivid tableau of a Viking funeral, ending with a badly charred model.

FITTINGS

Deckhouses and lifeboats can now be added to the ship.

DECKHOUSES

Take nine matchsticks and glue them together to form a block as shown. Cut the block to provide two sections of equal length.

Sand each section to shape, stain, varnish and paint. The tops are white.

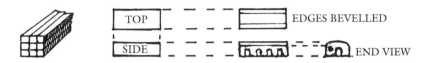

LIFEBOATS

Take a single matchstick and from it shape two small boats as illustrated. Stain and varnish the boats and paint them with light gray tops. Glue them side by side on top of one of the deckhouses.

To set the deckhouses on the ship, apply some varnish on the end of a wire to the deck just forward of the mizzen mast and the mainmast. Pin the deckhouse to be set in position on the end of a needle secured to a length of wire. Work the deckhouse inside the bottle and into position over the varnished spot and set it down in place.

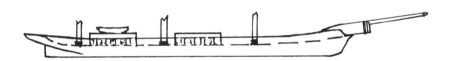

The bottle cap is glued and screwed on.

To leave their signature upon a successful work, some model-makers put their name on a piece of paper that is placed inside the bottle underneath the putty.

I prefer to write some verses on the paper, or perhaps a brief history of the ship that has been bottled — also my name, the date of completion, and the name of the person for whom the model has been made. This is then glued carefully on the outside of the bottle and covered with two coats of clear varnish.

Sometimes the bottle is stoppered with a cork and the air drawn out of the bottle with a syringe, and the cork sealed with wax. I have never used this procedure.

One of the most attractive ways to complete the model is to finish off with a Turk's Head knot around the end of the bottle neck.

THREE-PART TURK'S HEAD

The line is looped around the core as shown, and the short standing end may be temporarily taped down to hold it in place while reeving the long working end. About 6 feet (1.8 m) of cord line is required.

The bight is pushed to the right under *A* and the working end is rove through it and tucked over and under following the arrow in the diagram.

The working end is then tucked around successively over and under to form the desired number of turns.

Should you find that you are becoming tired, or irritable, or that your eyes are straining, set the work aside for a time; no sailor ever risked the ruin of his sight for the sake of a pastime. At one time a deck officer needed 20/20 vision without glasses, or he would find himself tramping the streets in search of the much-dreaded "shore job."

When I was sitting in my cabin in the old *Garvelpark* with its dark furnishings, peering at my progressing handiwork in the dim light while the steam winches wheezed and banged in the night outside, old Captain Johnston stopped by the door, "Good God, lad, ye'll ruin your eyes wi' that."

No ship in a bottle, however well made, was worth that price.

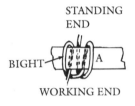

STANDING END

BIGHT   A

WORKING END

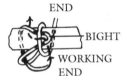

STANDING END

BIGHT

WORKING END

STANDING END

WORKING END

II. TRANS-ATLANTIC STEAM SAILING VESSEL

DIE HOLLAND-AMERIKA-LINE.

Life
That makes us keep on
  moving . . . . setting sail
For undiscovered anchorages.

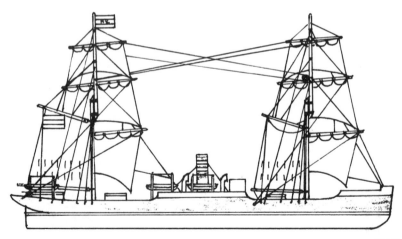

F.R.B.

The trans-Atlantic steam sailing vessel is in part modelled on the lines of the SS *Schiedam* of the Holland-America Line, *c.* 1880.

The *Schiedam* — 2,745 g.r.t. — was built in 1874 at Dumbarton, Scotland, as the *San Marcos* for the Liverpool & Texas Steamship Company.

In 1877 the Holland-America Line bought the vessel, which was renamed the *Schiedam*.

The *Schiedam* was sold to the Fratelli Cosulich Shipping Company in 1897 and sailed as the *Miramar* under the Austrian flag until being broken up in 1903.

The illustration on the previous page is to scale and may be used for measurements.

HULL

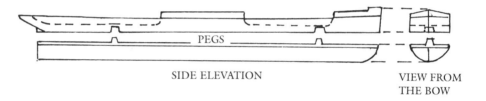

PEGS

SIDE ELEVATION

VIEW FROM
THE BOW

Because of the depth of the hull of this model, it must be made in two parts if it is to go down the neck of the bottle.

Small pegs must be fashioned and set in the bottom half (painted red with a thin white upper line) with corresponding holes being made in the top half.

The upper half of the hull (painted gray with white along the raised sections of the fo'c's'le and accommodation space), upon which the masts and rigging will be set up, is cut and shaped in much the same fashion as the full-rigged ship.

The holes for masts and threads and the recesses for the deck fittings are cut where shown.

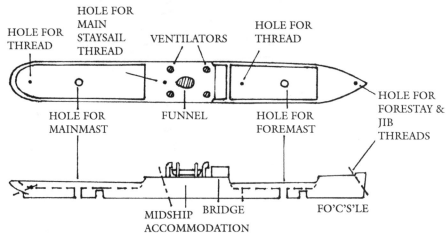

HOLE FOR THREAD   HOLE FOR MAIN STAYSAIL THREAD   VENTILATORS   HOLE FOR THREAD

HOLE FOR MAINMAST   FUNNEL   HOLE FOR FOREMAST

HOLE FOR FORESTAY & JIB THREADS

MIDSHIP ACCOMMODATION   BRIDGE   FO'C'S'LE

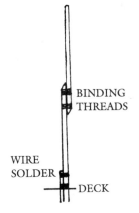

BINDING THREADS

WIRE SOLDER

DECK

MASTS

The masts are each in two parts, but fitted together, shaped and set up as for the full-rigged ship.

The yards and booms are made to proportion for the model as depicted in the illustration (actual size) on page 26.

The lower yard is the length of a standard wooden matchstick, and the two above are very slightly shorter.

UPPER TOPSAIL

LOWER TOPSAIL

MAIN/FORE SAIL

RIGGING

The rigging of the masts and yards follows the pattern for the full-rigged ship.

However, to rig the braces on the main upper topsail yard, the following procedure is used:

A small block is made by cutting out a piece of stiff cardboard. This should be as small as possible while accommodating two holes: one for pull-thread 2 by which the block is held against the foremast at the height shown, the other for the needle

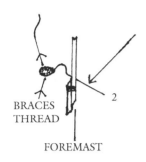

BRACES
THREAD

FOREMAST

2

threading the upper topsail braces for the mainmast to the fore-mast and back again.

To fit the block, attach one end of a long thread to the block. The other end is threaded with a needle through the foremast and down through the bow. Mark this pull-thread *2*.

The block should be stiffened with black paint, taking care to keep the needle hole clear so that the thread of the braces will run freely through it.

This thread must be free to run through the mast while the mast is being lowered before putting the model into the bottle.

If the thread of the braces is led through the foremast in the usual fashion it will be impossible for the masts to lie flat when putting the model into the bottle.

The fore upper topsail braces are rigged by threading them through the mainmast above the lower topsail yard as illustrated below:

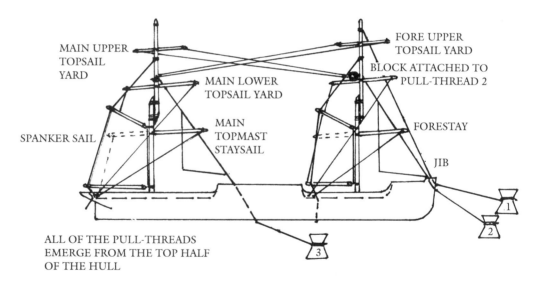

MAIN UPPER
TOPSAIL
YARD

FORE UPPER
TOPSAIL YARD

BLOCK ATTACHED TO
PULL-THREAD 2

MAIN LOWER
TOPSAIL YARD

SPANKER SAIL

MAIN
TOPMAST
STAYSAIL

FORESTAY

JIB

ALL OF THE PULL-THREADS
EMERGE FROM THE TOP HALF
OF THE HULL

Halyards and footropes are not shown in this diagram, although they would be rigged on the actual model.
There are only three pull-threads to this model.

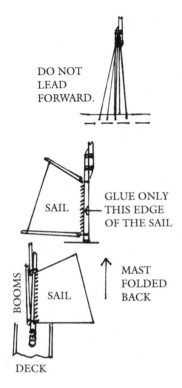

DO NOT LEAD FORWARD.

SAIL

GLUE ONLY THIS EDGE OF THE SAIL

BOOMS

SAIL

MAST FOLDED BACK

DECK

Caution: Never lead any of the shrouds forward of a mast, otherwise it cannot be laid flat.

SAILS

The square sails on the yards and the staysails and jib are made in the same manner as those for the full-rigged ship.

Fitting the spanker sails: These fore and aft sails on the fore and main masts may be fitted by cutting and coloring them as required and then setting them in place after the model has been put into the bottle.

OR

The spanker sails may be glued in place on the masts beforehand.

When the masts are laid horizontally before putting the model into the bottle neck, the spanker sail will be set out, "winged," to one side of the mast.

The sail will fold as it goes through the bottle neck, and it must be glued into position on the booms after the masts are fully raised inside the bottle.

FLAGS

— National ensign — Holland

— Company house flag — Holland-America Line

FITTINGS

Setting the upper deck fittings in place is perhaps the most difficult and painstaking task on this type of model.

These are:

 (i) Funnel and funnel stays
 (ii) Bridge/"dodgers"
 (iii) 4 Ventilators
 (iv) 4 Lifeboats
 (v) 2 Lifeboats — Upper deck, right aft.

Set on the raised midship section

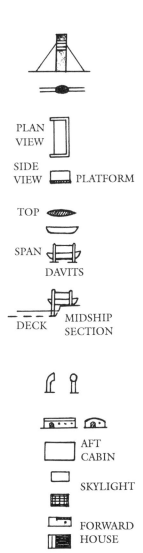

PLAN
VIEW

SIDE
VIEW — PLATFORM

TOP

SPAN

DAVITS

DECK   MIDSHIP
        SECTION

AFT
CABIN

SKYLIGHT

FORWARD
HOUSE

(vi) Deckhouses — Upper deck, fore and aft.

When they have been made, these pieces should be tried in place on the model before it is put into the bottle.

(i) The funnel is made from four matchsticks glued together then shaped and painted gray. The funnel stays (four) can be made from a matchstick shaved and sanded to a thread-like thickness and painted black.

(ii) For the bridge, make a very thin platform, stain and varnish, then set three weather "dodgers" around it at the front and to each side, painted white.

(iii) The lifeboats are shaped from matchsticks, stained and varnished, with light gray tops.

The davits are made from matchsticks shaved to very slender proportions and painted white. They are then glued in position on the outside of the lifeboat. The span is made from a matchstick shaved very thin and painted black.

The after-davit of the lifeboats at the aft end of the midships section is slightly longer, to reach to the main deck below.

(iv) The ventilators are shaped from matchsticks and painted light gray and black.

(v) The deckhouse fittings are made from matchsticks glued together, cut and shaped to the dimensions shown, stained, varnished and painted.

SETTING THE SHIP IN THE BOTTLE

The putty may be put into the bottle and painted to create the sea, and the bottom half of the hull set in place on the putty at a very early stage in the building.

When the upper half of the hull is ready to go into the bottle — without any of the deck fittings — the masts are cut and lowered, and the yards are pivoted as for the full-rigged ship.

The bottom half of the hull and its pegs are lightly glued with a white resin glue, then the upper half is put through the bottle neck and set on the pegs; the masts are raised while this is being done.

This operation must be performed quickly, otherwise the glue will set and the midships pull-thread *3* could be stuck and left hanging slack.

When everything is in order, the deck fittings in the suggested order of deckhouses, bridge, funnel, ventilators and lifeboats are put into the bottle on the end of a flexible wire and set in place.

The lifeboats at the stern may be very difficult to set in place without interference from the rigging; in some cases they may have to be left off the model.

No matter how experienced and skilled the model-maker may be, ingenuity and improvisation are the key factors to success in this craft.

Sometimes it was an ingenuity born of necessity; the bars in seaports invariably had their share of ships in bottles high on some dusty shelves. These were often enough ill-shaped bits of wood with some slack rigging and masts held on a loose thread, hastily contrived by broke and thirsty sailors who offered them in barter for drinks.

I was a small boy when I saw my first model, shown to me by a school friend whose father was a sea captain. His prized possession, ranking above all his other childhood trophies, was what appeared to be an old ale bottle of distorting thick green glass; but inside it was a ship. True, it was but a ship of sorts, heavy-sparred and loose-rigged and somehow stuck to the bottle in which some bilgy-looking water sloshed around; but it seemed magical to me.

From such dross could come the gold of dreams, and the best models are born of dreamers held by visions of great voyages and great adventures. They are inspired to capture the spirit of the sea and imprison it, like some genie of desire, in a bottle.

III. British Coaster/Passage Boat

SS *Gem* (1902)

BUILT: *South Shields, England in 1881 — Iron hull registered at Colchester, Kent, England.*
Length — 80 feet. Beam — 16 feet. : 20 H.P.

OWNERS: *Beckwith and Mills. Master: D. Francis.*
This 100-ton, ketch-rigged steamer was the last of the Colchester passage boats; from 1902 it ran in the London carrier service and the coastal trade to Holland until 1914, when it was taken over for Admiralty service.

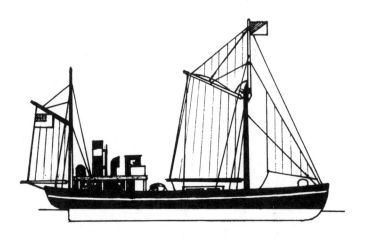

F.R.B.

S S GEM (1902)
The last of the Colchester passage boats

The old *Gem* is typical of John Masefield's "dirty British coaster with a salt-caked smokestack, butting up the Channel in a mad March gale."

The model of the *Gem*, the last power coaster out of Colchester, is made like the previous model of a steam sailing vessel in two halves pegged together.

While not as complex to construct as the larger types of vessel, the *Gem*, if made with attention to detail and well painted, makes a remarkably attractive model.

HULL

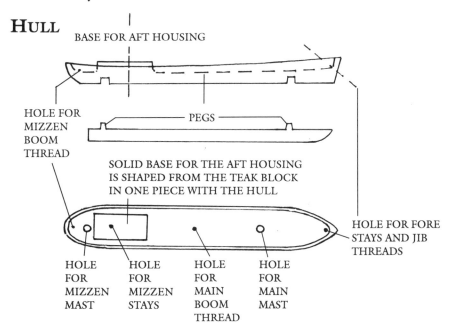

BASE FOR AFT HOUSING

HOLE FOR MIZZEN BOOM THREAD

PEGS

SOLID BASE FOR THE AFT HOUSING IS SHAPED FROM THE TEAK BLOCK IN ONE PIECE WITH THE HULL

HOLE FOR FORE STAYS AND JIB THREADS

HOLE FOR MIZZEN MAST

HOLE FOR MIZZEN STAYS

HOLE FOR MAIN BOOM THREAD

HOLE FOR MAIN MAST

MASTS

The mainmast is shaped from two matchsticks glued together in the same manner as for the other models.

The mizzen mast is splinted together to form a continuous piece.

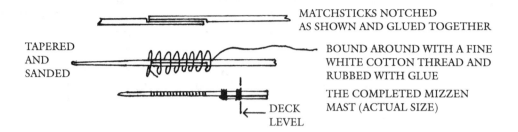

MATCHSTICKS NOTCHED
AS SHOWN AND GLUED TOGETHER

TAPERED
AND
SANDED

BOUND AROUND WITH A FINE
WHITE COTTON THREAD AND
RUBBED WITH GLUE

THE COMPLETED MIZZEN
MAST (ACTUAL SIZE)

DECK
LEVEL

Wire solder is bound to the masts and they are stepped in position like the masts of the previous models.

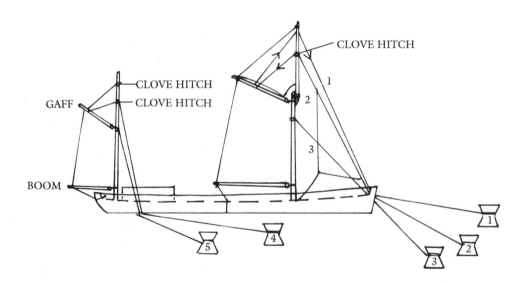

CLOVE HITCH

GAFF

CLOVE HITCH
CLOVE HITCH

BOOM

The booms and gaffs are shaped to the dimensions shown, attached to the masts in the usual fashion and rigged as described.

RIGGING

The rigging of the pull-threads follows a slightly different pattern in this model.

Take a long piece of thread — approximately 24 inches (61 cm) — and near the middle of its length tie it in a clove hitch where shown, half-way up the main topmast.

Lead one end of the thread down through the hole in the bow with a needle. Mark this pull-thread *2*.

Take the other end of the thread and with the needle thread it through the main gaff as illustrated. Lead it back up to the top of the mainmast through which it is then threaded with the needle. Finish by leading the end down and threading it through the hole in the bow. Mark this pull-thread *1*.

Pull-thread *3* is rigged in the usual fashion from the mainmast to the hole in the bow.

For the mizzen mast a thread is clove-hitched at the masthead. The end is led down and threaded with a needle through the mizzen gaff and back to the mast where it is again clove-hitched before being threaded through the hole behind the funnel position. Mark this pull-thread *4*.

Pull-thread *5* is rigged in the usual fashion from the mizzen mast to the hole behind the funnel.

The threads through the hull and leading to the booms and gaffs are rigged in the standard way.

The shrouds and stays are rigged like those in the previous models.

There are three shrouds and one stay on the mainmast, and two shrouds and one stay on the mizzen mast.

The mainmast gaff has guys running from its peak to the port and starboard bulwarks.

SAILS

The sails are cut and colored, then attached to the masts by glueing only the forward edge of each sail.

The jib is attached in the usual way.

When the masts are lowered to go into the bottle, the sails are "winged out" as described on page 30 for the model of the trans-Atlantic steam sailing vessel.

Company flag — The house flag on the mainmast is that of Francis and Gilders, who took over from the old firm of Beckwith and Mills.

FITTINGS

As with the model of the SS *Schiedam*, neatly made deck fittings are what give a polished finish to the *Gem*.

The bridge, wheelhouse and ventilators are made so that they may be set in place as one unit.

For this unit a thin platform must be provided, stained and varnished, and cut so that it will fit around the mizzen mast stays.

The wheelhouse, bridge "weather-dodgers," ventilators and stanchions are fitted on this platform.

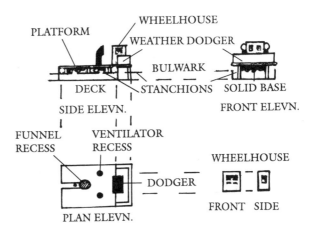

The wheelhouse, bridge "dodgers" and ventilators are made to the dimensions shown, in a fashion similar to that for the fittings for the SS *Schiedam*, then painted and glued in place.

The stanchions can be made from matchsticks shaved very thin, painted white, then glued in position

The platform with the wheelhouse, bridge "dodgers," ventilators and stanchions in place, and with a hole or recess cut for the funnel, is positioned on the solid aft housing base after the ship is in the bottle.

MAIN HATCH

The main hatch is made to the size shown, sanded and stained.

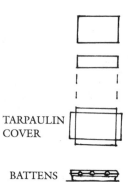

TARPAULIN
COVER

A tarpaulin hatch-cover is cut from paper as illustrated and painted with watercolors a dark bluish-green.

Cover the hatch with the tarpaulin by glueing down the edges of the paper over the hatch.

Make hatch battens from matchsticks, paint them black and glue in position around the four sides of the hatch.

BATTENS

Varnish the hatch, cover and battens completely, then glue in place on the deck before the ship is put into the bottle.

Of course, making fittings like this is miniaturist's work, but it is vastly more satisfying than merely painting the top of the hatch green. The same degree of fineness applies also to the next fitting.

SHIP'S BOAT

The ship's boat is shaped from matchsticks as shown, and stained.

40

Make a boat-cover from paper and paint it a dark bluish-green like the hatch tarpaulin, and fit to the boat. Varnish the boat and its cover.

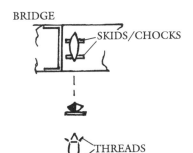

BRIDGE

BRIDGE

Two wooden skids are made, painted white and glued in place on the deck where shown, forward of the bridge and aft of the main hatch.

THREADS

The boat is glued in position athwartships on the skids and thin white cotton threads are passed over each end of the boat to the deck on either side before putting the ship into the bottle.

FRONT

SIDE

TOP

WINDLASS

The windlass is constructed from pieces of matchstick cut, put together and painted, then glued in place in the fore part of the ship before being put into the bottle.

FUNNEL

The funnel is made in the usual way and painted black with an orange band.

The steam whistle on the front of the funnel is made from a thin sliver of matchstick attached with light blobs of glue so that it will stand out from the funnel.

The whistle is painted black with a gilt top.

The funnel is set in place after the ship is in the bottle.

AFT DECKHOUSE

The aft deckhouse is quite straightforward, stained and varnished with a black top.

The deckhouse goes in place when the model is in the bottle.

SETTING THE SHIP IN THE BOTTLE

The bottle is prepared and the bottom half of the hull set in the putty in the same way as that of the SS *Schiedam* model.

When cutting the bases of the masts prior to lowering them, be sure to cut high enough that they will lie flat along the top of the solid aft housing base.

When the ship is in the bottle and the masts raised into position, the bridge and wheelhouse platform is put in place, then the aft deckhouse, and finally the funnel.

For effect, the sea may be built up at the rear of the bottle to tilt the hull forward and give the impression of a small coaster lurching before a fresh North Sea swell.

The men who sailed the coastal traders were fine seamen, and like seamen everywhere they were rogues of great resource, as any reader of W. W. Jacobs' tales in *The Nightwatchman and Other Stories* well knows.

My father had a staunch old Norwegian bosun who painstakingly made large models of sailing ships with a true sailor's concern for accuracy and detail. The detail was a masterpiece of deception. The upper deck was fitted with hatches that could be opened up and tightly closed to seal a hollow hull — which could be filled with contraband booze and thus concealed from prying port officials.

How many of the ships in bottles have been filled with neat spirits before being sealed and passed off to inquisitive customs officers as a memento of many quiet hours on a long sea voyage?

Nothing was too much effort if it provided a few cheap drinks.

IV. FRENCH TRADING VESSEL: MEDITERRANEAN, 18TH CENTURY

Now is the season of sailing; for already the chattering swallow is come and the pleasant west wind; the meadows flower, and the sea tossed up with waves and rough blasts has sunk to silence. Weigh thine anchors and unloose thy hawsers, O mariner, and sail with all thy canvas set.

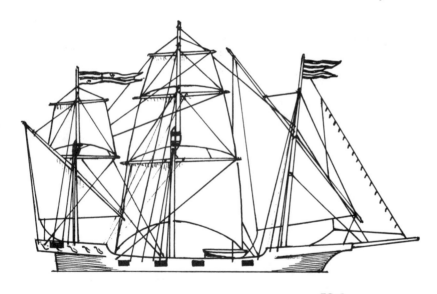

F.R.B.

POLACRE-XEBEC
Eighteenth century

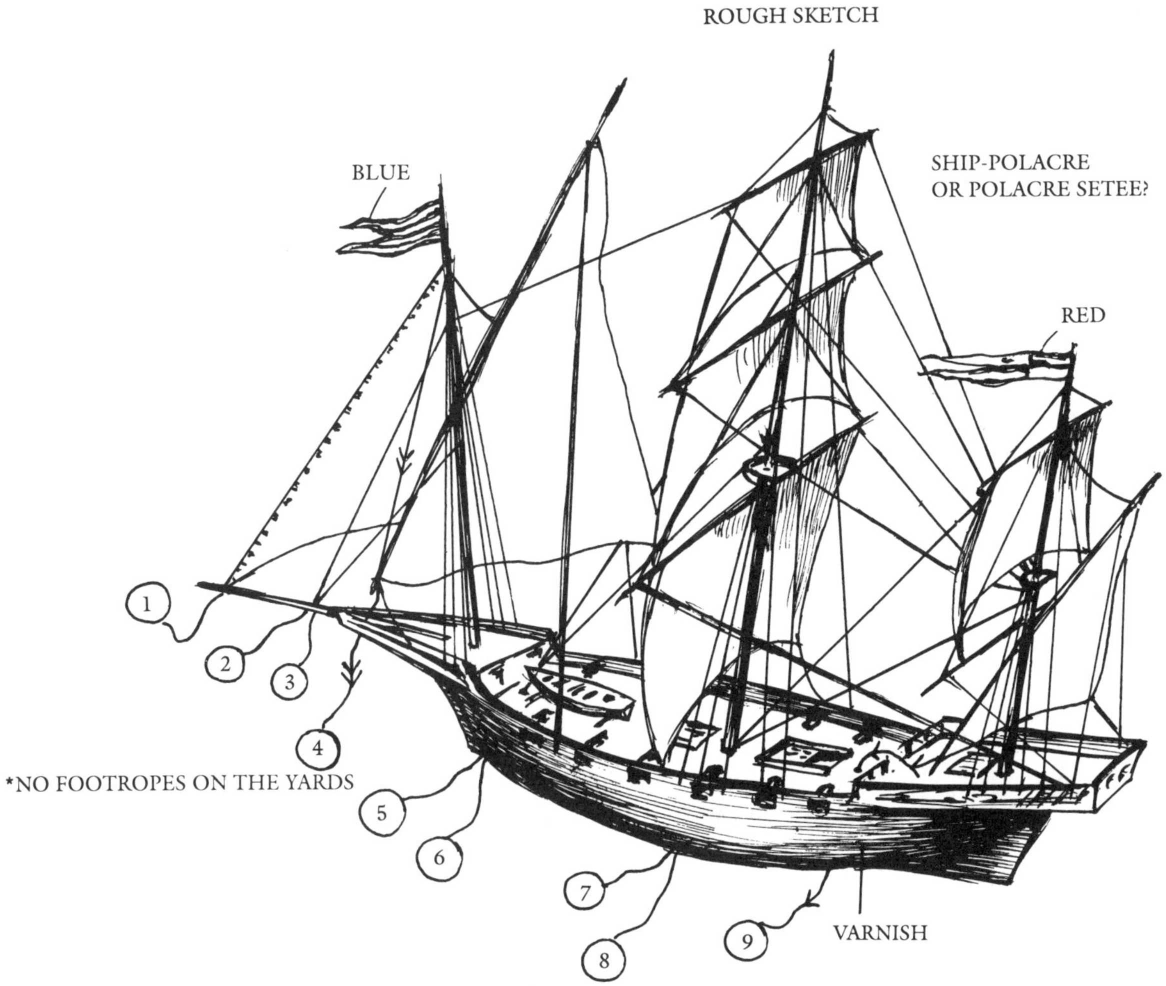

ROUGH SKETCH

BLUE

SHIP-POLACRE
OR POLACRE SETEE?

RED

①

②

③

④

*NO FOOTROPES ON THE YARDS

⑤

⑥

⑦

⑧

⑨

VARNISH

FRENCH - MEDITERRANEAN-1750S - FAST TRADING VESSEL - 18- GUN.
ARMED AGAINST PIRATES.

Some model-makers make preliminary sketches to get the feel of
the ship, and to develop ideas on how to approach the construction of their model.

Anybody who remembers the story of Robinson Crusoe will recall the xebec, the North African slaver and pirate ship propelled by sails and oars.

The xebec and the polacre were two similar types of craft found mainly in the Mediterranean, and arguments still go on today over the peculiar features of their rigs.

The xebec was narrow in the floor and broad in the beam, square-rigged on the foremast by some accounts, and with a lateen sail on the main and mizzen masts. Other definitions describe the more usual rig as lateen sails on all three masts.

The polacre of the eighteenth century, with its masts formed from single spars without crosstrees, was usually square-rigged on the mainmast with lateen sails on the fore and mizzen masts; sometimes this rig was called polacre-settee. Another variation of the rig had the mizzen mast in two pieces instead of a single spar. The largest vessels of this type could be as much as 1,200 tons.

Both were extremely fast craft, ideal for trade or treachery, and the xebec required a very large crew to handle its rig for full advantage from the slightest shift of wind.

HULL

The polacre-xebec was a low, sleek, rakish craft, so the hull can be shaped in one piece — narrow at stem and stern with slightly raised poop and fo'c's'le decks.

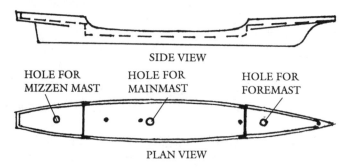

SIDE VIEW

HOLE FOR   HOLE FOR   HOLE FOR
MIZZEN MAST   MAINMAST   FOREMAST

PLAN VIEW

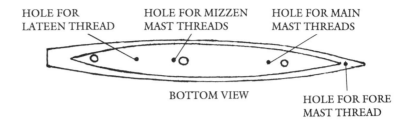

HOLE FOR LATEEN THREAD

HOLE FOR MIZZEN MAST THREADS

HOLE FOR MAIN MAST THREADS

BOTTOM VIEW

HOLE FOR FORE MAST THREAD

The entire hull is varnished and the insides of the bulwarks are painted white.

Gilt, red or blue-colored decorative designs may be painted on the raised portions of the stern and fo'c's'le if desired.

MASTS

The polacre was so called because its masts were formed from one piece, a single spar without crosstrees.

For this model, however, only the foremast has been made as one spar; the main and mizzen masts are in two pieces.

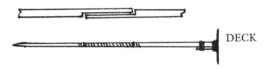

DECK

To make the foremast, two matchsticks are splinted together, shaped and bound with white cotton thread like the mizzen mast for the model of the SS *Gem*.

The foremast is raked forward and the mizzen mast is raked slightly aft, so the holes in the deck must be angled accordingly.

The mainmast and mizzen mast are each made from two matchsticks cut to the sizes shown and joined in the usual manner.

Yards/Spars

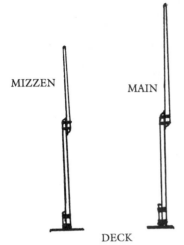

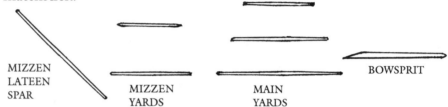

Splinted sections should always be well varnished, because there will obviously be a fair strain upon them when the masts are being raised inside the bottle.

The spar for the mizzen lateen sail can be made from a single matchstick.

MIZZEN LATEEN SPAR

MIZZEN YARDS

MAIN YARDS

BOWSPRIT

The main and mizzen yards are cut to the lengths shown. The bowsprit is made from a single matchstick.

Rigging

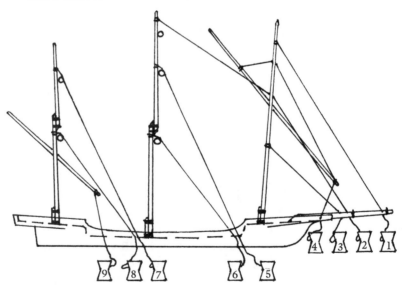

Although the rigging is not as detailed as that of the full-rigged ship, there are nine pull-threads for this model.

Pull-thread *1* runs from the head of the foremast down through the end of the bowsprit.

Pull-thread *2* is tied at the head of the mainmast and led down through the foremast above the lateen spar and out through the bowsprit.

Pull-thread *3* is secured approximately one-third of the way up the foremast and threaded through the bowsprit immediately behind pull-thread *2*.

Pull-thread *4* is tied approximately one-quarter of the length from the head of the fore lateen spar, threaded through the foremast and tied to the other end of the spar, and then threaded through the bowsprit *and* the apex of the fo'c's'le deck.

Pull-thread *5* is tied to the mainmast above the lower topsail yard and runs down through the main deck close aft of the break of the fo'c's'le.

Pull-thread *6* is led from above the main yard down through the same hole in the main deck as pull-thread *5*.

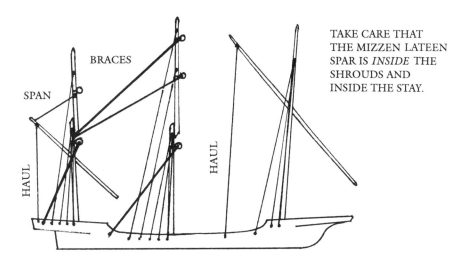

SPAN

BRACES

HAUL

HAUL

TAKE CARE THAT THE MIZZEN LATEEN SPAR IS *INSIDE* THE SHROUDS AND INSIDE THE STAY.

Pull-thread *7* runs from the head of the mizzen mast through the hole in the main deck behind the mainmast.

Pull-thread *8* is tied to the mizzen mast above the mizzen yard and led through the same hole as pull-thread *7*.

Pull-thread *9* is tied to the forward end of the mizzen lateen spar and threaded through the hole in the main deck just forward of the break of the poop.

The standing rigging is rove through masts and bulwarks as in the pattern for the full-rigged ship.

There are three stays on the foremast, three shrouds and two stays on the mainmast, three shrouds and one stay on the mizzen mast.

Hauls run from the peaks of both lateen spars to the port and starboard bulwarks, through which the threads are worked with a needle and tied in place. They are rigged in the same way as the guys on the mainmast gaff on the model of the SS *Gem*.

Halyards are rigged on all of the yards as for the full-rigged ship, and the braces are led through the mizzen mast and bulwarks following the same procedure. There are no braces on the mizzen top yard.

Great care must be taken when rigging the mizzen mast, because the holes in the bulwarks are so close together that the wood may be easily split, breaking off the bulwark. If in any doubt, reduce the number of shrouds/stays to two instead of the four shown.

A span is tied to the peak of the mizzen lateen spar and led to the mast close below the mizzen top yard where it is secured.

An added touch may be given to this model with downhauls of white cotton thread.

One set of downhauls is tied near the top of the foremast as shown, and the ends glued firmly to the break of the fo'c's'le 1/4 inch (60 mm) apart on either side of the centerline.

White threads are also attached to the main yard and the lower top yard on the mainmast, two to each yard and spaced 1/8 inch

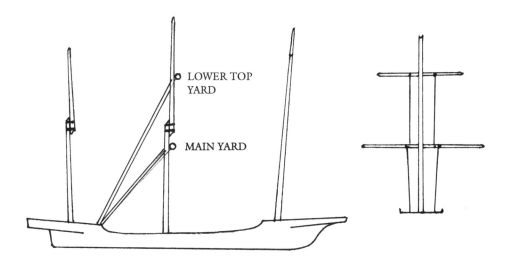

LOWER TOP
YARD

MAIN YARD

(30 mm) out from the mast. The ends are glued to the break of
the poop an equal distance from the centerline.

SAILS

The sails are cut to the patterns shown in the illustration on p.
44, tinted and glued in place on the yards and spars.

As the masts are lowered prior to putting the ship in the bottle, the haul threads from the peaks of the lateen spars will slack-
en and the spars will lie parallel to their masts. The lateen sails
should be lightly rolled so that they may be eased past the bottle
neck without being crushed and creased.

MIZZEN

FORE

FLAGS

The flags for this model have been chosen from colorful illustra-
tions of the period and may not be accurate historically. Some

model-makers may wish to research the types of flags flown by French Mediterranean trading vessels of the eighteenth century.

FITTINGS

The deck fittings on this model are fairly simple, and all of them may be set in place before putting the vessel into the bottle.

The deck cannons are the most obvious items of the deck fittings, and they are set against the inside bulwarks in line with the gunports on the outside. There are eight cannons on the main deck, two on the poop deck.

A large vessel of this type may have carried as many as eighteen guns, probably being engaged in the very lucrative silk trade between Lyons and the Levant and, therefore, a richly tempting prize for the corsairs and Algerine sea-pirates of the North African Barbary coast.

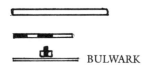
BULWARK

Take a matchstick length, shave it very thin to form the gun platform and paint it light gray.

The cannon lengths are made from another shaved-down matchstick, painted black and cut to size, then glued to their gray platforms or trunnions.

The assembled pieces are then glued in position on deck.

DECK

The ship's longboat is cut and shaped as in the diagram and set upon chocks that are positioned on the main deck forward of the mainmast. The longboat is stained and varnished and the top painted light gray. The chocks are painted white.

COAMING

DECK

The main companion hatchway is formed from a thin rectangle of wood surrounded on three sides by a high coaming. The hatchway is stained and varnished and set on the main deck where it is glued exactly between the hole for the lateen spar thread and the hole for the mizzen mast thread.

DECK

The main cabin hatch to the poop deck is simply a square piece of thin wood, stained and varnished with a gray center on top and glued in place on the poop deck between the mizzen mast and the break of the poop.

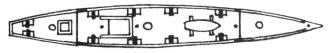

DIAGRAM SHOWING THE DECK FITTINGS IN PLACE.

SETTING THE SHIP IN THE BOTTLE

The masts are cut, lowered and the model put into the bottle in the same way as the previous models.

When the ship is in the bottle, the masts raised and the yards and sails set in position, a final touch may be put to the sails.

With long tweezers or a long flexible piece of wire, lengths of previously measured cotton thread may be inserted in the bottle and attached to the bottom corners of the mainsail with a light touch of glue. When the glue is firm, the loose ends of the thread are then led back with the tweezers/wire and glued to points on the outside bulwarks just forward of the break of the poop.

Similar threads or "sheets" may be attached to the aft lower corners of the triangular jib and lateen sails, with the loose ends being glued to the deck below.

I was making a model of the polacre-xebec with all going well enough until the masts were being raised inside the bottle. An extra strain on the pull-threads to haul taut the rigging caused the ship to lurch suddenly in its sea of putty. At the same time there was a sharp snap and the top of the foremast splintered and sagged forward as though the vessel had been struck by a sudden fierce gust of the northeast mistral that blows into the Gulf of Lyons.

It seemed a disappointing and frustrating climax to a venture that had been progressing well and was within a heaving-line's throw of a successful ending.

No sailor easily gives up his ship, and this one was not what Lloyd's would call a total constructive loss. The ship's head was brought around to course once more in its putty sea. Repairs were carried out by slipping a running bowline of light cotton thread over the foremast top. The bowline was hauled taut so that the fractured pieces were rove together then glued and varnished using the end of a length of wire.

When all was set, the thread was cut close to the mast with a fragment of razor blade in a stick and the pull-threads tightened; no blemish could be seen in the result, and the vessel was once more shipshape and Bristol fashion.

V. Barque-Rigged Arctic Whaler: 1890s

Ever they hear the floe-pack clear,
*   and the blast of the old bull-whale,*
And the deep seal-roar that beats off-shore
*   above the loudest gale.*

KIPLING

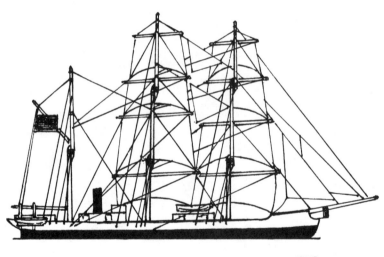

F.R.B.

Rough sketch for the model of a barque-rigged Arctic whaling ship. Two extra whaleboats could be set in davits on either side amidships.

Cumberland Sound in the fall of the year was the great place for whaling in the Canadian Arctic during the nineteenth century.

Scottish whaling ships from Dundee spearheading the Greenland whale fishery had their stations in the Sound at Blacklead Island and Kekerten Harbour.

American whalers like the one illustrated worked the northwest corner of Hudson Bay after 1860. By then steam was being used in addition to sail, and from the 1870s on most of the Eastern Arctic whaling ships had steam propulsion giving them greater speed and easier handling.

Whaling was virtually finished in the Canadian Arctic by the end of the first decade of the twentieth century. Kekerten Harbour and Blacklead Island were closed down around 1910, although the Dundee firm of Kinnes still had interests at Kekerten until the Hudson's Bay Company bought them out in 1923.

The whaling ships were remarkably tough and versatile craft. Typical of them was the old *Erik*. Built at Dundee, Scotland, in 1864, she was a barque-rigged steamship of 580 tons and sailed for seventeen years in the Greenland whale fishery until being bought by the Hudson's Bay Company in 1882.

The ship was again sold in 1901 to Baird's of St. John's, Newfoundland for the seal hunt. In 1902 and 1908 she served as a supply ship for the Arctic expeditions of Commander Robert Peary, USN.

The end came in August 1918, when the *Erik* was bound from St. John's to Sydney, Nova Scotia. The German submarine *U156* stopped and boarded her, then sank the old vessel with explosive charges.

HULL

The whaling ships were sturdy craft built for durability rather than style, neither as sleek nor as fine-lined as the clippers, and the hull is shaped accordingly.

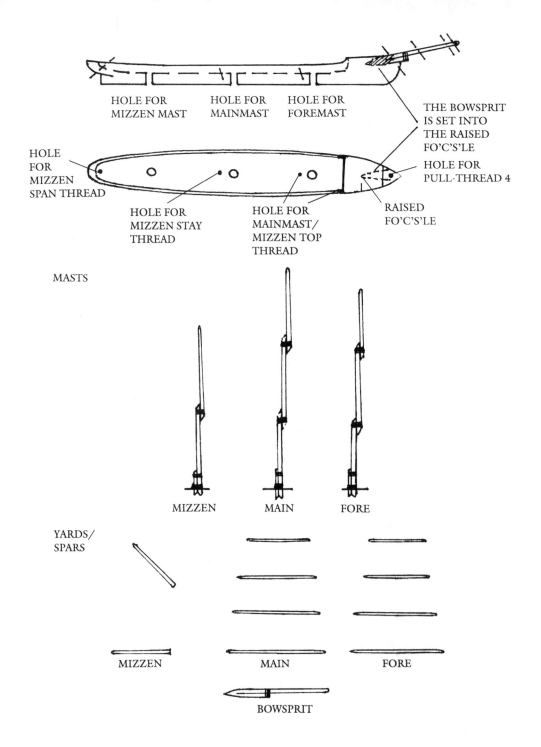

HOLE FOR
MIZZEN MAST

HOLE FOR
MAINMAST

HOLE FOR
FOREMAST

THE BOWSPRIT
IS SET INTO
THE RAISED
FO'C'S'LE

HOLE FOR
MIZZEN
SPAN THREAD

HOLE FOR
PULL-THREAD 4

HOLE FOR
MIZZEN STAY
THREAD

HOLE FOR
MAINMAST/
MIZZEN TOP
THREAD

RAISED
FO'C'S'LE

MASTS

MIZZEN   MAIN   FORE

YARDS/
SPARS

MIZZEN   MAIN   FORE

BOWSPRIT

RIGGING

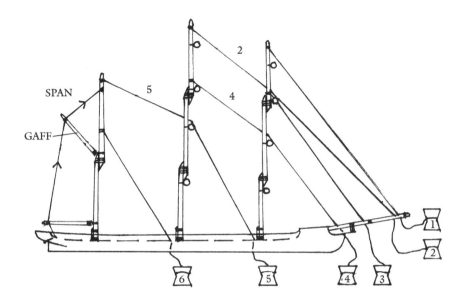

There are six pull-threads for this model:

Pull-thread *1* leads from the foremast head down through the farthest forward point on the bowsprit.

Pull-thread *2* leads from the mainmast head down through the foremast and through the bowsprit close behind pull-thread *1*.

Pull-thread *3* is tied to the foremast at the height shown and then led down through a point mid-way along the bowsprit.

Pull-thread *4* is tied to the mainmast at the height shown and led down through the foremast, through the bowsprit and the deck beneath and out through the bow.

Pull-thread *5* is secured to the head of the mizzen mast and led through the mainmast down through the hole in the deck close behind the foremast.

Pull-thread 6 is tied to the mizzen mast at the height shown and led down through the hole in the deck close behind the mainmast.

The thread for the mizzen span is knotted at one end and the other end led through the hole in the stern, knotted around the lower boom and led to the gaff, around which it is again knotted and then tied to the mizzen top at the height shown.

The standing rigging of shrouds and stays is threaded through the masts and bulwarks in the fashion described for the model of a full-rigged ship.

There are three shrouds and two stays on the fore and main masts; two shrouds and two stays on the mizzen mast.

The yards are rigged with halyards and braces in the same way as those of the full-rigged ship model. Footropes were not fashioned for this particular whaling ship model, but they may be rigged in the usual manner if desired.

There are no braces on the topmost yard of the mainmast for the reason that when rigged on this model the brace will not run freely through the mizzen mast, in spite of using a fairly fine, well beeswaxed thread. Rather than strain the mast and probably have it break while being raised inside the bottle, the reluctant thread is cut away to leave only the halyards on the yard.

Whaling ships were work-horse vessels. They had about them none of the expensive finishings of Clyde-built ships, nor the Aberdeen clippers' smartness aloft where the blocks were made so small that the running gear was very heavy to work.

SAILS

The sails are cut to the patterns shown in the illustration on page 56, tinted and glued in place on the yards and mizzen.

The fore and aft sails on the mizzen mast are fixed in position like those on the mainmast on the model of the SS *Gem*.

A whaler's sails had a gray, worn look. They were not the scrubbed canvas wings of a crack Yankee packet boat, but work-stained by the rigors of their trade.

FLAGS

The United States' flag is one in which the number of stars/stripes varies at different times in the country's history.

There are generally seven red and six white stripes.

FITTINGS

All of the deck fittings and the ship's boats are set in place after the model has been put into the bottle, although they must be tested in position before the hull is put inside.

DODGER

FUNNEL RECESS

DODGER

BRIDGE HOUSING NOTCHED SO THAT THE WEATHER "DODGER" AND PLATFORM MAY BE FITTED IN PLACE

The weather "dodger" is built around a thin platform that is then fitted and glued into a notch cut in the fore part of the bridge housing.

Midships boat — set on skids placed on top of the forward deck housing.

Aft deck housing — placed between the mizzen mast and the hole for the mizzen stay thread.

Funnel

Forward deck housing — placed between the mainmast and the hole for the mainmast/mizzen top thread.

After whale boats — these are placed right aft on either side with the davits outside the bulwarks in the fashion of the New Bedford whaler.

SETTING THE SHIP IN THE BOTTLE

The sea in the bottle should be very dark like the waters of Hudson Bay, with patches of putty painted white to represent loose ice and bergy bits awash in a transparent foam.

When the model has been set in its sea and everything is in order, the deck fittings are put in place in the following sequence: aft deck housing, bridge housing/weather "dodger", funnel, forward deck housing with the boat on top, after whale boats.

During his years of sailing in the Arctic, my father knew an elderly character named Du Val who lived near Pangnirtung in Cumberland Sound.

Du Val was an American who, as a young man, had sailed in the whaling ships that hunted the finback and white wales in the headwaters of the Sound. He had been well acquainted with the legendary whaling captain George Comer who charted part of Southampton Island.

A harpooner, Du Val was disabled by a white whale that he had successfully struck. The whale plunged away at high speed with the whaleboat in tow, but the harpoon line ran foul. In an attempt to clear the mess of rope Du Val's right arm became entangled in the line and was torn completely from its socket.

In 1926, Du Val took a trip to the States for "one last look at civilization." On his return he gave my father his opinion of it as, "Too many gol-durned cars." He preferred the isolation of the North.

These whaling men do not seem to have much favored the bottling of ships. Their great pastime for idle hours was scrimshaw work, the carving and coloring of designs on ivory or whalebone.

VI. The Nonsuch: *17th-Century Ketch*

And north, amid the hummocks,
   A biscuit-toss below,
We met the silent shallop
   That frighted whalers know;
For, down a cruel ice-lane,
   That opened as he sped,
We saw dead Hendrick Hudson
   Steer, North by West, his dead.
                              KIPLING

The NONSUCH — *ketch, seventeenth century*

To provide some idea of the size and scale of a vessel of this type, the following are some of the approximate measurements that might be found:

Length to end of bowsprit - 75'
Mainmast from keel to truck - 80'
Length - 50'
Mizzen mast - 50'
Breadth - 16'
Main yard - 34'

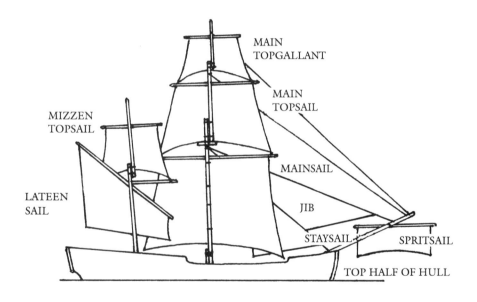

Sail Plan of the *Nonsuch* - (Not to scale)
A model of these dimensions would fit very snugly into a "pinch" bottle without any top clearance.

ROUGH SKETCH

THE "NONSUCH"
17TH-CENTURY KETCH
50 TONS

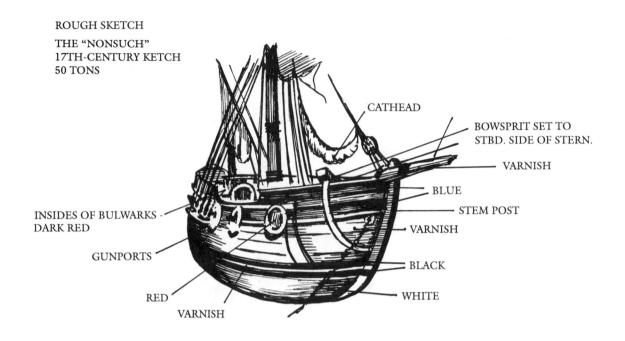

CATHEAD

BOWSPRIT SET TO
STBD. SIDE OF STERN.

VARNISH

BLUE

STEM POST

VARNISH

BLACK

WHITE

INSIDES OF BULWARKS -
DARK RED

GUNPORTS

RED

VARNISH

LEFT GRAVESEND, - 3 JUNE, 1668
ANCHORED OFF RUPERT RIVER - 29 SEPTEMBER, 1668
- WINTERED IN JAMES BAY, AT FORT CHARLES

CAPTAIN ZACHARIAH GILLAM OF BOSTON

REACHED ENGLAND - 10 OCTOBER, 1669 - WITH CARGO OF
FURS, THAT "MADE THEM SOME RECOMPENCE FOR THEIR
COLD CONFINEMENT".

Rough sketch and history of the ketch *Nonsuch* of 50 tons in
which Médard Chouart, Sieur des Groseilliers, sailed to James
Bay and provided the foundations for the Hudson's Bay
Company of England.

The voyage of the tiny *Nonsuch* into Hudson Bay was indeed a great adventure and a great achievement. Arriving there in the fall of 1668, after her consort the *Eaglet* had been dismasted and forced to turn back for England, the crew wintered in quarters set up on the ruins of a house which had been built there years before by the English. This house was probably the one built by Henry Hudson's men sometime in 1611. After a "cold confinement" there the *Nonsuch* was sailed back to reach London in October 1669.

The memory of the *Nonsuch*'s epic voyage was revived with a replica built to sail across the Atlantic for the three-hundredth anniversary. A Canadian stamp was issued in June 1968, also to commemorate the occasion. Such a vessel provides a worthy challenge to model in a bottle, and as a result of the publicity there are now enough pictures to be found upon which to base the drawings for a model.

From the numerous pictures and photographs a model was designed for a 710 mL "pinch bottle" — a project that carries with it a fair risk. The model is deceptively simple, but its detail is so intricate and the fit so tight in the bottle neck that the slightest misjudgment will mean a failure. The proportions are such that if the hull is to be of a respectable size then the mainmast, if in scale, will when raised scrape the inside of the bottle.

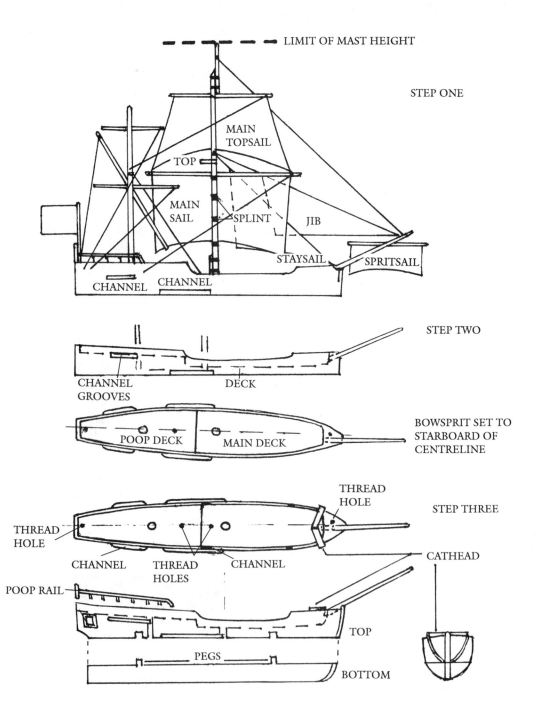

LIMIT OF MAST HEIGHT

STEP ONE

MAIN
TOPSAIL

TOP

MAIN
SAIL

SPLINT

JIB

STAYSAIL

SPRITSAIL

CHANNEL

CHANNEL

STEP TWO

CHANNEL
GROOVES

DECK

POOP DECK

MAIN DECK

BOWSPRIT SET TO
STARBOARD OF
CENTRELINE

THREAD
HOLE

STEP THREE

THREAD
HOLE

CHANNEL

THREAD
HOLES

CHANNEL

CATHEAD

POOP RAIL

TOP

PEGS

BOTTOM

The development and construction of this model is described step by step without any reference to the full-rigged ship model, from which it is quite different.

Step One took shape in a drawing designed from old prints and pictures showing a bulky craft with main and maintop sails set. The rigging would require channels into which the shrouds could be fitted rather than being threaded through the bulwarks as done in other models. The mainmast would be longer than the average wooden match and so would need some form of splinting if it were to be made from matchsticks.

In Step Two a more detailed drawing was made of the top half of the hull which must be in two halves because the vessel sits high in the water and has a marked rise to the poop deck. The positions of the grooves for the rigging channels and the cut-out of the deck levels were drawn approximately to the form illustrated in pictures of the *Nonsuch.*

Step Three was a final refinement of the drawing in Step Two. The poop deck was lengthened slightly, the channels altered and the masts set farther forward. The bottom half of the hull was drawn with its pegs and their corresponding sockets in the top half. The raised stern-piece or "half-moon" with its poop rails was designed as a separate part. A shallow V-shaped cathead was set in the forward end of the vessel.

With the basic plan established, the building of the model was begun and carried out in the order now described.

COLOURING OF BOTTOM HALF OF HULL

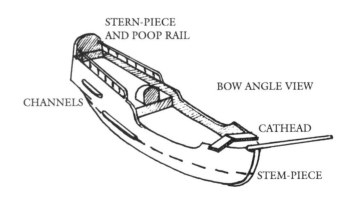

STERN-PIECE AND POOP RAIL

BOW ANGLE VIEW

CHANNELS

CATHEAD

STEM-PIECE

Hull

The top and bottom halves of the hull are cut and shaped to the dimensions shown in the drawing for Step Three. The bottom half is stained, varnished and painted as in the illustration — a very delicate task.

The bowsprit is made from a single matchstick, stained and glued in position, being set into the solid part of the bow, starboard of the centerline. By shaving a matchstick very finely, the stem-pieces are made and fitted to the top and bottom halves of the hull.

The channels are fitted into grooves in the hull, the bottoms of the forward pair of channels being flush with the bottom of the top half of the hull.

This must be done very exactly and checked for fit in the bottle neck — it will be a very tight fit indeed.

The channels are stained and the top half of the hull is oiled.

When the paint on the bottom half of the hull has dried, the putty sea, perhaps with an ice effect like that in the model of the Arctic whaler, is put into the bottle and painted, and the bottom half of the hull is set in place upon it.

Masts

The masts must be the next step, starting with the mainmast. Photographs of the *Nonsuch* replica showed this to be in three sections, the bottom one long and the top one small and very slender. To reproduce this in the model the bottom section is splinted. A maintop is fitted where the bottom and mid sections are joined.

The mizzen mast is made in two sections.

The masts are stained and varnished, and when dry the maintop section of the mainmast is rigged with shrouds.

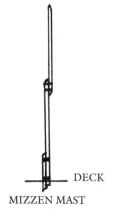

DECK

MIZZEN MAST

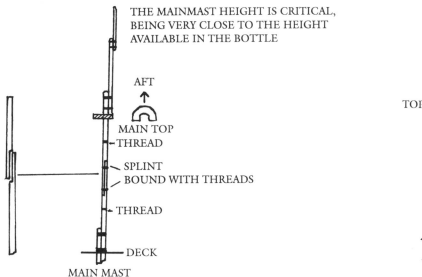

THE MAINMAST HEIGHT IS CRITICAL,
BEING VERY CLOSE TO THE HEIGHT
AVAILABLE IN THE BOTTLE

AFT

MAIN TOP
—THREAD

SPLINT
BOUND WITH THREADS

THREAD

DECK
MAIN MAST

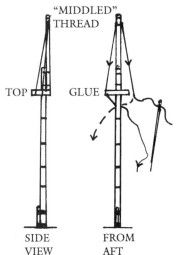

"MIDDLED"
THREAD

TOP   GLUE

SIDE   FROM
VIEW   AFT

TWO
SHROUDS
EACH
SIDE

A length of black buttonhole-twist is "middled" by threading it through the mainmast close to the head of the mid section.

One side of the thread is led down and glued to the outer edge of the top and the end threaded through the mast close below the top.

The procedure is repeated with the other side and the loose ends are cut off close to the mast.

A second thread is then rigged in the same way to provide a pair of shrouds on the maintop, both of them leading at an angle aft.

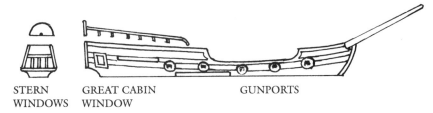

STERN   GREAT CABIN   GUNPORTS
WINDOWS   WINDOW

Two blue bands are painted around the top part of the hull as shown in the illustration. The insides of the bulwarks are painted a dark red.

HULL FITTINGS

The fittings are now made for the top half of the hull.

STERN WINDOWS

Although these are not reproduced with the detail of the original, the effect is created by glueing very finely shaved pieces of matchstick in the positions shown on the stern of the vessel.

GREAT CABIN WINDOWS

These, too, are made from thin slivers of matchstick glued at the after part of the hull on both sides.

STERN-PIECE AND POOP RAIL

The stern-piece and poop rail are cut and assembled as shown. Matchwood shaved very thin can be bent to the curve of the forward ends of the rails which are glued into small recesses made in the stern-piece with a pin or a finishing nail. The posts are tiny pieces cut off a sliver of match and carefully glued on the undersides of the rails. These posts are painted a dark red and the rails and stern-piece stained.

STERN LANTERN

The stern lantern is made from a match splinter bent to shape and with a light blob of glue added to form the lantern top, painted black with a white lantern. The piece is glued into a small notch cut in the center of the stern-piece which, with rails and lantern, is varnished completely.

GUNPORTS

Gunports are cut from stiff cardboard. The center part is painted red to represent the actual gunport and the outside border is painted with a metallic leaf finish for a wreath effect. The gunports, five to each side, are glued in place where shown in the diagram.

STOCK
SHANK
FLUKES

ANCHOR CATHEAD

The anchor cathead is made to the size shown in the drawing for Step Three, stained and glued in place.

ANCHOR

The anchor is made from pieces of match and painted black. It is glued in place with one fluke resting on the main deck, the other against the aft end of the cathead and the stock outside the starboard bulwark.

A small piece of thread may be attached to the outboard end of the shank and hung down in a bight to be glued at a point — painted with a small black dot — close to where the bowsprit and stemhead meet.

The entire top half of the hull is varnished when the gunports, windows and anchor have been glued in place.

YARDS/SPARS

Cut and shape the yards and spars for the main and mizzen masts as shown:

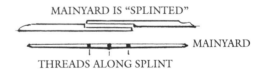

MAINYARD IS "SPLINTED"

MAINYARD

THREADS ALONG SPLINT

The mainyard, because of its length, must be made from two matchsticks splinted together, glued and tightly bound with threads.

There will be considerable strain on this yard, and so it is advisable to test it for strength before going any further, to avoid a break at some later, more critical stage.

When completed, the mainyard is stained and varnished.

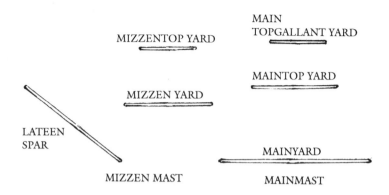

MIZZENTOP YARD

MIZZEN YARD

LATEEN
SPAR

MIZZEN MAST

MAIN
TOPGALLANT YARD

MAINTOP YARD

MAINYARD

MAINMAST

Some prints and drawings of the *Nonsuch* were found showing the vessel with three sails set on the mainmast, and not two as had been at first imagined. A main topgallant yard was added to make a total of three yards on the mainmast.

The yards are stained and varnished and set aside to dry.

The mainmast is "stepped" — glued firmly into its hole in the main deck.

RIGGING

The shrouds, stays and pull-threads are all rigged with black buttonhole-twist thread.

The shrouds are rigged to the channels on the hull on either side of the masts. There are five shrouds and one stay on the mainmast, three shrouds and one stay on the mizzen mast.

The shrouds are rigged one pair at a time. A length of thread is threaded through the mast with a needle and "middled."

One end of the thread is glued in a notch made with a razor in the fore end of the channel on one side of the hull. When that end is firmly held, the thread is pulled taut and the other end glued in a corresponding notch in the channel on the opposite side.

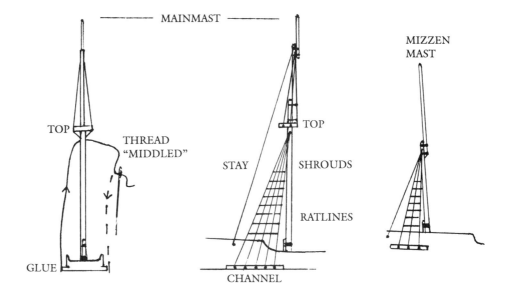

This procedure is repeated with the other pairs of shrouds at equal intervals along the channels.

The stay is rigged by knotting one end of a length of thread which is threaded through the bulwark from the inside outward and led up through the mast — on the mizzen it is put through the same point as the three shrouds — and down through the opposite bulwark from the outside inward where it is pulled taut and glued in place.

Ratlines are fitted by glueing short lengths of light brown embroidery thread across the shrouds and trimming the ends.

When the mainmast has been rigged with shrouds and stay, the mizzen mast is "stepped" in its hole in the poop deck with a slight rake aft.

The mizzen mast is rigged with its three shrouds and stay in the same way as the mainmast.

There are six pull-threads on this model.

Pull-thread *1* runs from the head of the mainmast to the farthest forward point on the bowsprit.

Pull-thread *2* is tied just below the main topgallant mast and led forward through the bowsprit close behind pull-thread *1*.

Pull-threads *3* and *4* are combined in a long piece of thread "middled" on the mainmast below the top. One end of the thread is passed with a needle through the bowsprit a short distance behind pull-thread *2*. This end is pull-thread *3*. The other end is led through the hole previously made in the solid part of the bow (see the drawing for Step Three) and brought out through the bow at the stem-piece. This end is pull-thread *4*.

Pull-thread *5* is tied just below the mizzen topmast and led down through the hole in the main deck close aft of the mainmast.

Pull-thread *6* is rigged after the mizzen lateen spar has been tied in position.

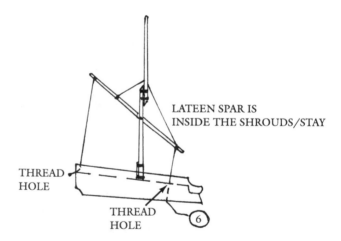

LATEEN SPAR IS
INSIDE THE SHROUDS/STAY

THREAD
HOLE

THREAD
HOLE

6

The lateen spar is tied to the mizzen mast at the point shown. A thread of buttonhole-twist is knotted at one end and threaded through the hole made in the stern (see the drawing for Step Three) to be tied at the peak of the lateen spar.

HALYARD THREAD

FOOTROPES

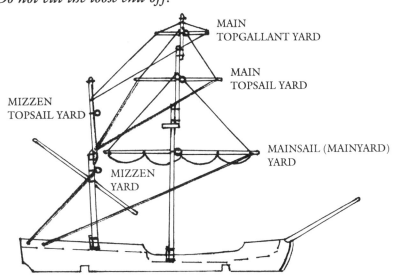

Pull-thread *6* is knotted around a point one-third of the length from the spar peak and with a needle threaded through the mizzen topmast at the height shown and down through the hole previously made in the poop deck (see the drawing in Step Three).

The mainyard is rigged with a length of light brown #50 sewing thread gathered in bights to form the footropes, with the loose end left free to be rigged as a halyard later.

Do not cut the loose end off.

MAIN
TOPGALLANT YARD

MAIN
TOPSAIL YARD

MIZZEN
TOPSAIL YARD

MAINSAIL (MAINYARD)
YARD

MIZZEN
YARD

The mainyard is tied in place at the height shown and the loose end of thread is threaded through the mainmast at a point close above where the main topsail yard will be tied. From there the thread is led to the other end of the mainsail yard, pulled taut, tied and glued at the end of the yard, to form the halyard. The loose end is cut off.

The braces are made from stone-colored buttonhole-twist thread. One end of a length of thread is tied to an end of the mainyard and led aft to the point shown, where it is threaded through the bulwark across the poop deck and out through the bulwark on the other side. From there it is taken to the other end of the mainyard, pulled taut, tied and glued in place.

The main topsail yard is rigged in a similar manner, except that it has no footropes.

The main topgallant yard braces and halyards are made entirely with light-brown #50 sewing thread. Buttonhole-twist was thought to be too heavy for the slender mizzen topmast, and would probably not "run" smoothly through the mast when pivoting the yard in preparation for putting the model into the bottle; it could easily break the mizzen mast.

The mizzen yard is rigged like the mainsail yard with halyards of #50 sewing thread and braces of buttonhole-twist. There are no footropes. The braces are led through the bulwarks and across the poop deck at a point close aft of the braces for the mainyard.

The mizzen topsail yard is tied to the mast at the height shown and rigged with halyards only.

The spritsail yard is cut and shaped from a matchstick at this stage, stained and varnished. When dry, it is rigged with footropes of light-brown #50 sewing thread.

The spritsail yard is tied to the bowsprit close *behind* pull-thread 3, the knots being made so that it can pivot like the yards on the masts.

Halyards of #50 sewing thread are rigged so that they will run from one end of the spritsail yard to the other through the bowsprit between pull-threads *1* and *2*.

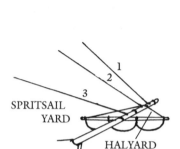

SPRITSAIL YARD

HALYARD

YARD IS TIED TO THE BOWSPRIT *BEHIND* PULL-THREAD 3

SAILS

The sails are cut to the patterns in the illustration on page 000. They are voyage-weary gray canvas, worn and stained by endeavor and accordingly tinted. The sails are glued in place on the yards, lateen spar and spritsail yard. There is no sail on the mizzen yard; mizzen topsail only.

DECK FITTINGS

The fittings for the main deck are made: main hatch, ship's boat and cannons.

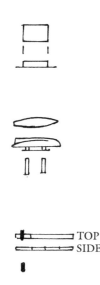

MAIN HATCH

The Main Hatch is a rectangle cut from matchsticks, stained, varnished and glued in place on the main deck between the mainmast and the anchor flukes.

SHIP'S BOAT

The Ship's Boat, shaped from matchsticks, is painted white and placed in a keep-up position on chocks that are glued across the main hatch.

CANNONS

The Cannons carried in the *Nonsuch* were small pieces more capable of sound than of fury.

The bases or trunnions of the cannons are cut from lengths of shaved matchsticks painted dark red.

The cannons are cut from thin lengths of matchstick painted black and glued on the trunnions — six pieces in all.

These pieces are glued on the main deck with the cannons against the bulwarks in line with their gunports, three to each side, forward of the mainmast.

SETTING THE SHIP IN THE BOTTLE

The ship is put into the bottle in the usual way with the masts cut near the foot and lowered, and the yards and spars pivoted to lie in a line with them.

This is a more than usually tricky job with the *Nonsuch*, because of its extremely tight fit in the bottle neck. The ship has to be forced past the neck with considerable pressure. Once inside, the head of the mainmast will touch the inside of the bottle, and the long mainyard must be trimmed to a fair slant because it stretches beyond the available width in the bottle.

Setting the top half of the hull upon the bottom half already inside the bottle must be done quickly, as with the model of the SS *Schiedam*.

FITTINGS SET IN PLACE INSIDE THE BOTTLE

When the masts have been raised completely, the stern-piece with its attached lantern and poop rails is worked into position.

This particular procedure is the one to be used where the model requires an extra deck, as would a galleon. The additional poop deck for a galleon would probably be a solid piece with bulwarks and, therefore, pressed into position without too much trouble; but the *Nonsuch*'s is open with side rails that are easily snagged in the rigging.

The piece is maneuvered into position by dangling it vertically on the end of a flexible wire until it can be slipped down between the shrouds on either side to sit on the bulwarks. The great virtue of patience is handsomely taxed by this endeavor. To make it easier, one rail may be removed, and when the stern-piece is in place this rail is passed down the bottle neck on a wire and set in position separately. The ease is relative; this method is still very demanding of patience.

ENSIGN

The staff and ensign to be flown from the stern are now made. The staff is cut from a thin-shaved length of matchstick, stained and varnished. When dry, the ensign is glued to the staff and the piece passed down the bottle neck on the end of a wire and glued in place at the stern; another awkward task. The ensign and staff must go down the bottle neck at an angle and then be brought to the vertical to be set in place against the stern-piece.

TILLER

SIDE

TOP

This is made from a very thin sliver of matchstick bent to the shape shown and glued to a tiny portion of matchstick, stained and varnished. The piece is glued in position on the stern-piece next to the ensign staff.

"HOOD"/DOORWAY AT THE BREAK OF THE POOP

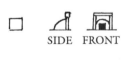

SIDE   FRONT

TOP

This piece is cut and shaped from matches and assembled to the form shown, stained and varnished. The completed piece is put into the bottle on the end of a wire and glued in place at the fore end of the poop deck between pull-threads 5 and 6.

BELAYING RAIL

This stand for the pins for belaying the running rigging is made from three thin pieces of matchstick glued together in the form of a Π . Although normally stained and varnished, this one was painted white for color effect and set in position amidships, close forward of the mainmast.

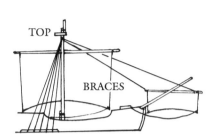

If desired, a finishing touch is given to this model by the addition of brace-hauls for the spritsail yard.

Threads may also be attached to the lower corners of the spritsail and led back to the cathead to be glued into place.

Another thread is led from the lower starboard corner of the mainsail back to the main shrouds where it is glued to the bulwark.

How often as a small boy on a damp, depressing, raw Glasgow day would I stand peering through the streaming windowpane of one of the great shipping companies, enthralled by a meticulously detailed model from their fleet of the kind made by Messrs. Bassett-Lowke. In all its glory of detail and company colors and gleaming brass fittings it brought the romance of far-off places to the drab Glasgow streets, evoked the sounds and scents of distant lands and made old sea-stories come alive.

Another favorite haunt in youth was the marine museum section of the Kelvingrove Art Gallery in Glasgow. Everything was there from Bassett-Lowke models to miniature carved-bone frigates made by nineteenth-century French prisoners-of-war. One model was so tiny, rigged with human hair, that it sat permanently under a magnifying lens. There was by contrast beside it a huge model of a sailing ship, its rigging faultless in its myriad detail but its underwater hull-shape clumsy and ill-proportioned; obviously the work of a seasoned old topman or bosun.

Also in Glasgow was a spot called The Argyle Arcade that had a hobby and crafts shop with the ringing name of The Clyde Model Dockyard. In its widow, one day, there appeared a remarkably neat model of a sailing ship in a bottle set among the many expensive and sophisticated scale model kits of almost every imaginable craft from dhows to luxury liners.

These were perhaps the only times in my life when I knew envy; if only I could make models to equal these. I loved them for their exquisite detail, their cleanness of line, their evocation of the spirit of the sea. And more than anything I wanted to make models of as many types of vessels as possible and somehow put them into bottles; a guaranteed lifetime challenge. The size of the bottles would obviously limit the possibilities of making an exact scale model, but at least something of the reality might be captured to delight the boy eternal.

VII. SCHOONER ALTERNATIVE

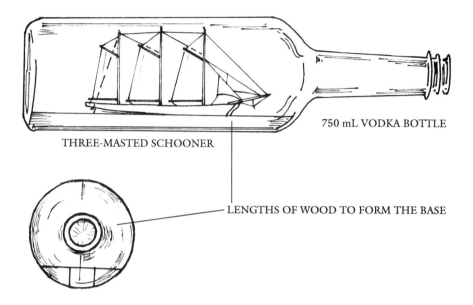

THREE-MASTED SCHOONER

750 mL VODKA BOTTLE

LENGTHS OF WOOD TO FORM THE BASE

A simple, neat and consequently very attractive model in a limited range of options can be made by using a slightly different method of construction.

For this type of model a standard round-bodied, long-necked bottle, such as a 750 mL vodka bottle, is used.

The base for the model inside the bottle is constructed from three lengths of wood shaped to the contours of the bottle, stained or painted as desired, and glued together inside it to form a level sea-base.

This wooden base is covered with a sea painted on paper that is then rolled up, passes down the neck of the bottle and glued at the top of the base.

Instead of painting a sea, suitably colored paper or possibly an appropriate sea from a magazine photograph may be glued on the base.

The rig for this type of model is limited to fore and aft only, because the masts are folded forward to go into the bottle — not backward as done with the other models — and so there can be no standing rigging of shrouds and backstays.

The attractiveness of this model must, therefore, be at the expense of realistic detail.

HULL

The model-maker has a greater scope for the dimensions of his ship because of the variety of bottles available, than could be had with the standard 710 mL or 750 mL pinch bottles used for previous examples.

Consequently, the dimensions shown in the following diagrams should serve only as a general guide.

The hull can be carved from any soft wood, even balsa, and a stem-piece shaped from balsa to fit the bow.

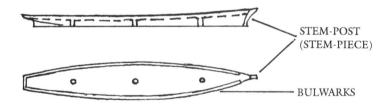

Because there are no stay/shrouds, the bulwarks may be shaped separately from thin strips of balsa and glued in place.

MASTS

The masts and the bowsprit may be shaped out of single pieces of wood.

There will not be any pull-threads passing through the bowsprit, and so a "dolphin striker" may be fashioned and fitted in place as shown.

The bases of the masts have pieces of thin fuse wire attached to their core ends in this model, because the masts are folded forward.

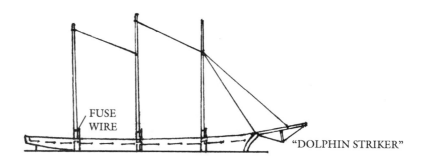

Lengths of thread are secured to the masts and bowsprit to form the fore and aft rigging, and a short piece of thread leads under the bowsprit to the "dolphin striker" in the form of a **V**.

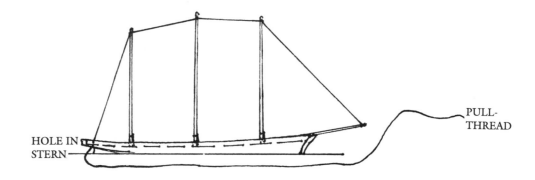

There is only one pull-thread required on this model. A length of thread, approximately one-and-a-quarter the length of the bottle, is tied at the end of the bowsprit. The thread is then secured to the peaks of the fore, main and mizzen masts and led down through a hole in the deck at the stern of the ship, leaving a long loose end that will hang out of the neck of the bottle.

SETTING THE SHIP IN THE BOTTLE

The masts are notched as before, except that they are cut at the back, not the front, and folded forward to lie flat along the deck.

Glue is applied to the area where the ship will sit in the bottle.

The model is passed down the neck of the bottle and set in position on its base, care being taken that the pull-thread can run freely.

When the model is firmly set in its place, the masts are raised gently to the upright position with the help of a long wire or probe, and by the pull-thread. Light touches of glue are applied to hold everything in place, and the pull-thread is cut off close to the hull at the stern.

FITTING THE BOOMS AND SAILS

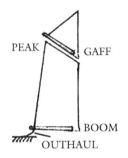

PEAK / GAFF

BOOM

OUTHAUL

The sails are cut to shape and colored; the gaffs and booms are made and glued to their respective sails, which are kept as separate pieces.

Each mast is lightly glued down one side when its sails are ready to be attached. The lower sail is loosely rolled and passed down the bottle neck to be put in place on its mast.

The top trysail is then similarly set in its place, and the peak of the lower sail is glued to the gaff.

The sails may be set at any desired angle. Thread "outhauls" can be glued to the end of the boom and to the deck below by careful use of a long wire inside the bottle.

The jibs may be fitted either before or after the model goes into the bottle.

FITTINGS

As with the previous types of model, small deck cabins and hatchways and boats may be cut from balsa wood and painted to provide fittings for the deck.

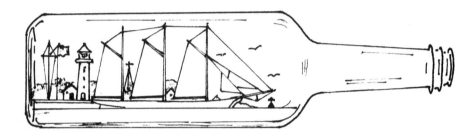

Bottles of this style were used on occasion by nineteenth-century sailors for displays of great ingenuity and contrivance. Entire seaport towns might be built inside the bottles as background to the ships, with piers, lighthouses, churches and buoys; sometimes a landscape and sky would be painted on the back of a bottle. Seagulls were even displayed, set on very fine wires cunningly camouflaged.

I have always made my models while serving on board a ship, using whatever materials came to hand; there was always an abundance of paint and putty.

Putting ships into bottles is a distinctly individual skill, and every practitioner has his own hoard of favorite techniques and tricks.

The time required to make a good model, including the sketches and the drawing of plans, can range from eighty to 200 consecutive hours, depending on the degree of detail desired. The full-rigged clipper ship will take between 160 and 200 hours. This is a skill that is plied for love, certainly not for money.

Here are some, but by no means all, of the alternatives to the methods described in the previous pages:

STAPLE

(i) Masts — These may be cut without any wire solder or other stiffening at their bases. This is a very risky procedure and depends for its success upon the quality of the wood used to shape the masts.

Another method for lowering the masts is to use a ∏ – shaped wire staple as a hinge at the base of the mast.

While being rigged, the masts should be held firmly in place with a small wedge driven between the base of the mast and the deck. Where the rigging is very detailed, like that of the clipper ship, this method is not recommended because the pulling and straining involved may very easily slip the heel of the masts off the wedge.

(ii) Fittings. — The range of modelling materials is much widened by an availability of hobby shops. Fittings may be made from balsa wood that is very easily cut and shaped. Light cardboard can be cut and assembled and stiffened with nail varnish as another alternative.

(iii) Sea. — Instead of putty, colored plasticine may be used to make the sea in the bottle, the model being glued in a trough made in the plasticine before the ship is set inside.

(iv) Sometimes the models, if of steamships and therefore without any complications of rigging, are made by building the entire vessel bit by bit upon the hull inside the bottle. Each part is made and painted and then placed in position using a pair of long tweezers.